MUTTS

America's Dogs

MUTTS

America's Dogs

by Brian Kilcommons and Michael Capuzzo

WARNER BOOKS

A Time Warner Company

ⓦ Warner Books, Inc., 1271 Avenue of the Americas, New York, NY 10020

A Time Warner Company

Printed in the United States of America

First Printing: November 1996

10 9 8 7 6 5 4 3 2 1

LIBRARY OF CONGRESS CATALOGING-IN-PUBLICATION DATA
Kilcommons, Brian.
Mutts: America's dogs / Brian Kilcommons and Michael Capuzzo.
    p.   cm.
    Includes bibliographical references (p.   ) and index.
    ISBN: 0-446-51949-9
    1. Dogs—United States. 2. Dogs—United States—Anecdotes.
    3. Dogs—Training—United States. I. Capuzzo, Mike. II. Title.
    SF426.K49   1996
    636.7'00973—dc20   96-7881
                                                         CIP

Book design by Kathryn Parise

MUTTS

America's Dogs

by Brian Kilcommons and Michael Capuzzo

WARNER BOOKS

A Time Warner Company

w Warner Books, Inc., 1271 Avenue of the Americas, New York, NY 10020

A Time Warner Company

Printed in the United States of America

First Printing: November 1996

10   9   8   7   6   5   4   3   2   1

LIBRARY OF CONGRESS CATALOGING-IN-PUBLICATION DATA
Kilcommons, Brian.
Mutts: America's dogs / Brian Kilcommons and Michael Capuzzo.
    p.   cm.
    Includes bibliographical references (p.   ) and index.
    ISBN: 0-446-51949-9
    1. Dogs—United States. 2. Dogs—United States—Anecdotes.
    3. Dogs—Training—United States. I. Capuzzo, Mike. II. Title.
    SF426.K49   1996
    636.7'00973—dc20   96-7881
                                                                CIP

Book design by Kathryn Parise

This book could not have happened without Sarah Wilson, gifted dog trainer and writer, with Brian Kilcommons, of some of the best books written about dogs and cats. Or without the support of Roger and Jill Caras, Rachel Lamb, Hope Ryden, Mitch Douglas, Diana Loevy, Christopher Hull, Don Nathanson, Mark Kram, Chris Boyd, Bruce Boynick, and, most of all, the love and inspiration provided by Teresa Banik, Grace Caroline Capuzzo, Julia Isabella Capuzzo, Texas, Daisy, and Briar.

To them this book is dedicated.

—Michael Capuzzo

CONTENTS

PART ONE

The World's Greatest Dogs

Janet and Madison

INTRODUCTION:
A RALLYING BARK FOR MUTTS

Congratulations! And the warmest welcome we know of (wag-wag) to the first book ever about, presumably, YOUR DOG. If you already own one of the most popular dog types in America, such as the Black Dog, White Dog, or Benji-Type Dog, you're already in on the secret, part of the family. If you're thinking of adopting one of the more than one hundred mixed-breed dogs described here, such as the Collie-Shepherd or the Golden Retriever–Lab or any of the distinguished genus types known collectively as America's dogs, this is the book for you.

Mutts are simply the greatest dogs in the world. Most of the beloved pet dogs in America are, in fact, mixed breeds. Most dogs in all the world are mutts. Yet this is the first book devoted entirely to mixed breeds, their selection and training, their magical place in our homes and hearts.

This is the first book that tells deeply human dog stories about mixed breeds only: the Collie-Chow who awakened a boy from a coma with a single, loving lick; Old Yeller; the Pepsi Retriever; the absurdly wonderful Bassetdor, product of an affair between a Basset Hound and a Labrador, who looks like a Lab in a funhouse mirror; the Junkyard Dog that Ralph the junkman has etched on his heart for all time. We hope these are some of the most remarkable dog stories, about ordinary folks and their extraordinary mongrels, you will ever read.

But there are other important reasons for *Mutts: America's Dogs.* Think of this book as a warning bark, like the chorus the dogs of London sounded when Pongo and Perdita and ninety-nine Dalmatian pups were sentenced to spots on Cruella De Vil's coat. Every year in the United States, more than eight million wonderful mixed-breed dogs are needlessly destroyed. We've betrayed our best friends.

Most of these dogs, given a second chance, would be wonderful family members, as friendly, smart, healthy, and even-tempered as the costliest purebred. (Often, in fact, friendlier, smarter, healthier, and more even-tempered.) So why do tens of thousands of Americans spend $500 and up on dogs who are often more troublesome and less worthy? Because no one knows what to look for in a mixed breed, or how to predict their behavior. People are afraid of "secondhand" dogs. This book replaces fear with knowledge and compassion; we'll tell you all you need to know to fall in love with a mixed breed.

Go to your local animal shelter. Trust that nature, and the miracle of hybrid vigor that created our American democracy, produces better stock than faulty human-controlled breeding, which produced the British royal family.

Take this book under your arm and study the rows of dogs greeting you excitedly (wag-wag, wag-*wag, wag-wag!*) from their cages. Find one you like. Find one who likes you. Read the description of the mutt type to make sure his traits are suitable for your family. And take him home.

Thus will begin your own wonderful mutt story, which we sincerely hope you'll write and tell us someday, as this would make us very happy. Wag-wag.

McFly

Liz Sharpe

A Special Note on Breeds and Breeding

If you choose a mutt, please adopt from one of the thousands of excellent animal shelters in this country and instantly have your dog spayed or neutered. You will save a life, help ease the pet overpopulation crisis, and reduce the demand for breeds that creates so many sloppily bred purebred dogs doomed to short, sickly, unhappy lives.

If your heart's desire is a purebred, such as a Golden Retriever, we encourage you to carefully research the health and temperament problems common to many purebreds; and to adopt a purebred from an animal shelter (plenty of Goldens are there!) or from the incredibly devoted people who run breed rescue societies (you can get their number from your local animal shelter). If you must buy a puppy,

Mutts We'd Like to See

In May 1992, the *Mensa Bulletin* asked its readers to turn their big brains to the subject of mixed-breed dogs. Here are some of the best they came up with, according to *Good Dog!* magazine.

The Bulldog–Shih Tzu cross. A Bullshitz.

Boxer–German Shorthaired Pointer. A Boxershorts. A dog never seen in public.

Alaskan Malamute–Whippet equals a Mutepet. All bite and no bark.

Water Spaniel–Bedlington Terrier. A Waterbed dog. A good swimmer, but sleeps a lot.

Beagle-Keeshond. A Beeg Kees. Gives sloppy proof it loves you.

Borzoi-Chihuahua. A Borzhua. Middle-class dog.

Husky-Collie. A Hussie. The bitch down the street who's always in heat.

Husky-Mastiff. A Huff. Perenially annoyed dog.

Malamute-Pointer. A Moot Point. Owned by . . . oh, well, it doesn't really matter anyway.

Deerhound-Terrier. A Derrière. True to the end.

The Collie-Malamute. The Commute. A dog who lives on the subway.

The Spaniel-Doberman. The Spam. Such a mix no one knows what's in it.

The Norwich Terrier–Maltese. The Normal. Just a plain ol' dog.

The Pekingese-Dachshund. The Peking Dach. Owned by Chinese restaurants.

The Samoyed–Norwich Terrier. A Samwich. A dog not well bred or poorly bred, but between bread.

A Pointer–Irish Setter. Pointsetter. Traditional Christmas pet.

A Kerry Blue Terrier–Skye Terrier. Blue Skye. A dog for optimists.

Smooth Fox Terrier–Chow Chow. Smooch. A dog who loves to kiss.

The Labrador Retriever–Curly Coated Retriever. Lab Coat Retriever. The choice for research scientists.

Newfoundland–Basset Hound. The Newfound Asset Hound. A dog for financial advisors.

Dalmatian-Collie. The Dali. Surrealistic dog.

Babie

Norma Davis

Mastiff–Bengal Tiger Crosses

In the fifth century B.C., when the Persian King Xerxes overran Greece with his fearsome Indian war dogs, the Greeks trembled at the sight of these massive mongrels. The Greeks—who knew from drama—reported the mutts were crosses between Mastiff bitches and stud tigers. The Greeks were not completely wrong. Mastiffs can have a brindle coloration with felinesque black stripes over red and tan.

screen breeders as if they were your daughter's first boyfriend. Avoid pet shops and their mass-produced puppies altogether.

If you're seeking a Golden Retriever–Shepherd cross, or any of the dogs described in these pages, take heart. The shelter has many to choose from, at bargain prices. Totally verboten would be to *breed* the mixes described in this book. There are already far more dogs in the world than homes for them, and the absence of meddling gives mutts their special charm. A mutt is a masterpiece of nature. To breed one would be like running off a bunch of prints.

The M-Word: A Short History of Misunderstanding

Mutts, of course, is the generic term covering many popular types of dogs, which historically divide into two general categories: (a) mongrels, mixed breeds, mixes, and other names that appear to be derived from the *Esquire Gentleman's Cocktail and Liquor Handbook,* and (b) cross-breeds, crosses, half-breeds, hybrids, curs, and other terms that John Wayne could have used in *The Sands of Iwo Jima* but sound more like racial slurs today.

Tuffy

Evelyn Roper

Lucy

L. McGarry/C.Kokinas

cur 1. A mongrel dog, esp. a worthless or unfriendly one. **2.** A low, despicable person.

We are not making this up. ("Cur" is most effectively paired by our great writers with "homely," as William Styron illustrates poetically in *A Tidewater Morning:* "I envied their abandoned slovenliness, their sour unmade beds, their roaches, the cracked linoleum on the floor, the homely cur dogs leprous with mange that foraged at will through house and yard.")

We cannot change the history of the language. However, to the owners of beloved mixed-breed dogs, there is no higher, more poignant, richer, sentimental word than *Mutt*. Mutt owners are happy and flattered to have their dogs called *mutts*, so long as this construction is not used:

"Oh, he's *only* a mutt."

Mutts are the original dog, the dog who befriended humankind, the dog from whom all the current breeds were developed. The Irish have a saying, "The world

Yes, there's a built-in bias in our language against mutts. One need look no further than the *Random House College Dictionary:*

mutt (slang) **1.** a dog, esp, a mongrel **2.** a stupid person (short for muttonhead; a dolt).

mongrelize to subject to crossbreeding, esp. with a breed or race considered inferior.

Eddie

Ira Weissman

Chelsea

Linda Caamaño

is made of the Irish and people who wish they were." This is literally true of dogs. The dog world is made of mutts and dogs who wish they were. Given their choice, and a little privacy, purebred dogs after several generations would revert to the original dog, which is a forty-pound Brown Dog.

The dogs you'll find in these pages have been at the White House, served in our wars, guided the blind, starred on TV shows, stopped illegal drug smugglers, and won Frisbee contests. All of them are just plain mutts, meaning simply the most wonderful thing in their owners' lives.

And yet the most terrible things are said about mutts every day, unanswered. There are no Westminster Dog Shows to show off the finest mixes, no award-winning public relations staff to tout their virtues, no certificates of authenticity, no *brand-name identification,* which is of course the kiss of death in a consumer society. Yes, this is the central problem that dooms Heinz 57-Type dogs. Nobody makes money off them. Nobody has an investment to protect. People just love them.

They're just our dogs.

What the heck kind of dog they *really* are even their owners often don't know.

Our goal is to help end this confusion. Flip to the pages ahead and you're bound to find your dog, or at least a close facsimile, described for the first time.

But first, telling their story requires setting the record straight on a few matters.

HYBRID HEROES

First of all, mutts aren't just common but often uncommonly brave. Any dog-lover reading the following stories will come away deciding proudly, "My dog is 100% mutt!"

🐕 All Hail Blackie

It was a very good year for heroic hybrids. Bailey, a Chesapeake Bay Retriever–Labrador Retriever mix, saved his owner from a raging bull and was named the 1996 Ken-L Ration Dog Hero of the Year. You can read his remarkable story in the Sporting Mutts chapter. But save some applause for Blackie, a humble mix from Lowell, Massachusetts, who was a runner-up in the Ken-L Ration contest. In December 1995 Blackie alerted his family to a fire in a vacant house across the street. Two weeks later, on Christmas night, a major fire erupted in Blackie's house. He ran from room to room, nuzzling sleeping children and tugging on their hair. He woke up ten people in all, giving everyone time to escape.

🐕 Tango Saves the Day

Al Choate, an auto mechanic from Port Townsend, Washington, was attacked by a mad mother cow who punctured one of his lungs and broke some ribs. Tango to the rescue! Tango, a mixed-breed Collie puppy, bit into the cow's cheek and didn't let go until Al had crawled to safety. When Tango won the Ken-L Ration Dog Hero award, Al's wife said, "She's just a wonderful dog, the best friend we'll ever have."

🐕 First Mutt in Space

When humankind decides to bravely go where no person has gone before, we send first . . . a dog. So it was in 1957, the dawn of the Space Age. Scientists had figured out how to launch human beings into satellite orbit but weren't sure how Earth creatures would endure zero gravity. On November 3 of that year, they sent a mutt to find out.

The first Earthling in space was Laika, a sweet-looking two-year-old Samoyed-Husky mix. She was strapped into a Soviet rocket and monitored by television and wires attached to her body.

Laika flew for six days in space. Alas, science didn't have the capability then to bring the dutiful little mongrel back alive, and she died, a martyr, when her masters shut off her oxygen supply from Earth. But enough was learned so that future space mutts—and astronauts—could come back alive.

🐕 Long Live the King

King, a German Shepherd–Husky mix, gnawed through a plywood door to save Howard and Fern Carlson from their burning house in Granite Falls, Washington. King's coat was in flames, but he stayed in the inferno until his heroic act was complete. "He was the last to leave," said Fern. "He wouldn't budge before we were outside."

🐕 Mixed-Breed Angels

Some dog experts will tell you that a Blue Heeler mix isn't a safe bet around children. Others will say a dog with Dachshund in it isn't a likely candidate for heroism. Still others insist dogs aren't capable of protective feelings for humans; they just act on instinct. No one says such things around Johnny Carlisle Coffey of Cassville, Missouri.

One cold spring day in the Ozark Mountains, ten-year-old Josh Carlisle pulled a baseball cap over his sandy hair, put on a thin red coat, and went to play in his backyard. Twenty minutes later, Josh's mother, Johnny, glanced out the window and felt her heart freeze. Her boy was gone.

"Josh!" she called to the silence of the deep woods beyond the family home on the outskirts of Cassville. "Josh!" By seven o'clock that night, in bone-chilling cold, a massive search was on, driven by an extra urgency. Josh has Down's syndrome.

More than seven hundred volunteers from Missouri, Kansas, Arkansas, Oklahoma, and West Virginia poured into the mountains in pickup trucks and off-road vehicles, planes, helicopters, on horseback and trailing bloodhounds. Nothing.

After two days and nights that plummeted to thirty-four-below wind chill, searchers talked about finding the body. "My mind was telling me there's no way he can be alive," said Johnny. "But my soul kept telling me, 'Don't worry, he's alive. Somewhere.'"

On the second night, Oscar "Junior" Nell of Springfield, Missouri, a fifty-year-old father, turned to his wife, Shirley, and said, "I'm going to Cassville to find that little boy." In 1989, their son, Tommy, had been killed in a car accident in Kansas City. "I just have to help," Oscar said.

Late that night, Oscar—wearing a gray cowboy hat and riding a steel gray mare—entered the woods and set up camp next to a small pond. At daybreak on the third day, he climbed on Perfection's Toot Toot—his mare with "a heart of gold," Oscar says—and led a search party of ten others into the woods.

The riders separated to cover more ground. Alone deep in the forest, Oscar and Toot followed a dry riverbed. "I couldn't see or hear anybody," Oscar said. But Toot seemed edgy, her ears perked. The horse wanted to go back in the other direction.

When the riverbed ended, Oscar finally heard what was frightening his horse. Barking. Two small dogs began running down the bluff toward Oscar and Toot, then ran back up the bluff. One was a Blue Heeler mix, the other a tiny Dachshund-Beagle mix, who ran around the horse's legs.

Oddly, the dogs were leading him toward a pile of trash on the hill. Something red flashed in the sun. Red! Fifty feet away, Oscar saw the black boots. "Oh my God," he said. "This is him."

"I got up to the place where he was lying, facedown," Oscar told the *Kansas City Star*. "Very, very lifeless."

"Josh?" he said. No response. The police had instructed him not to touch the body.

"Josh?" Slowly, the little boy raised his head, blinked, and managed a weak smile. When Oscar asked him if he wanted to go home, Josh said, "Uh, huh."

Oscar put Josh up on the horse and carried him across several miles of rough, mountainous terrain. At the top of the mountain was a house. Oscar called police. As rescuers put Josh in an ambulance to take him to a helicopter, the Dachshund-Beagle raced her little legs at top speed to follow the ambulance. "It was like she was saying, 'I've come this far, and now you're going to leave me,'" said one dog handler. Miraculously, Josh had suffered only frostbitten toes. The two dogs had snuggled against him in the night, keeping him warm. Josh, who can't remember or describe his experience, has adopted his rescuers, Baby and Angel.

"There's no other way you can look at this than as God's way of protecting him," Johnny Coffey is fond of saying, and no one disputes her. "Those dogs were angels."

🐕 The Miraculous Lick

On November 4, 1991, Donny Tomei, an eleven-year-old boy, was hit by a car and suffered a serious head injury. He lapsed into a deep coma.

For two weeks the medical staff at New Haven Hospital in Connecticut tried everything. Donny lay unconscious in a nest of IV tubes, unable to open his eyes or utter a word. Doctors sounded grim: half the people with such serious head injuries die. Many never recover.

Then one day Donny's dog, Rusty, a Chow Chow–Collie puppy Donny had adopted from a shelter, came to visit. Before anyone could react, Rusty raced by the medical staff, leapt onto Donny's chest, and licked him on the face.

Donny Tomei opened his eyes for the first time since the accident and smiled. Then he said, "Bad Rusty." These were the first words the boy had spoken. Dr. Charles Duncan, his neurosurgeon, stammered, "Donny is clearly not in a coma now."

The health benefits of dog companionship are well known, but even dog experts had never heard of such a thing.

Hundreds of cards and balloons and more than $3,000 in donations for Donny arrived, and many people sent pictures of their dogs. Pet stores offered dog food and a life-

time's grooming for Rusty. "This is really a-boy-and-his-dog story," Dr. Duncan said.

Donny's condition began to improve markedly after his family got permission to bring his beloved mutt to the hospital. That day, after uttering his first words, he ate for the first time since the accident.

"Rusty is my best friend," Donny said proudly. "I'll love him always."

Mixed-Breed Dogs Die Needlessly Every Day

This is a hidden national tragedy. The massive detainment and euthanasia of America's unwanted dogs costs taxpayers millions of dollars per year.

Added to this colossal waste is the spiritual cost of killing man's best friend. The periodic slaughter of wolves, dolphins, or other wild creatures brings international outcry and is said to diminish our humanity; the annual slaughter of millions of equally intelligent dogs is routinely accepted, though dogs are "emotionally the most humanlike" of all animals, as the great Harvard biologist E. O. Wilson told us recently.

Every day in this country, parents with young children confront a choice—what kind of dog for our family?—armed with *misleading or all the wrong information.* Too often, they pass on these worthy but doomed dogs in favor of a purebred.

All too often mutts from the pound are feared as an unknown quantity, unpredictable, risky, "somebody else's prob-

lem," sickly, aggressive. After all, what can a $25 dog really be worth?

Instead, soothed by image and prestige of purebred dogs and dog shows, families spend $500 and up for an American Kennel Club–registered dog.

What these families frequently end up with is a poorly bred and sickly specimen of German Shepherd, Cocker Spaniel, or Golden Retriever, a genetic wreck compared to what breeders and fanciers intended, destroyed by unethical breeding and profiteering.

In many cases they would have been better off with a mutt. Mixed-breed dogs are what nature intended of dogs—and are on the whole healthier, often more intelligent, of more even disposition, and live longer lives than many purebred dogs. This is due to what geneticists call hybrid vigor. Mixed-breed dogs are often the superior, economical, moral, and ethical choice.

Mutts: The Invisible (Not Silent!) Majority

The common misconception is that pure-bred dogs are the most popular canines in the United States.

Golden Retrievers, Labradors, Dalmatians, Saint Bernards, Collies, German Shepherds, et al. dominate our magazine advertising, television shows, fashion layouts, new movies, and old stories. They leap to mind when we wonder, "What *kind* of dog should I get?" because historically they have been the *only* kinds described.

You need only to walk through virtually any American neighborhood on a Sunday morning, trace the barks and howls to their source, and you will see the truth, the common wisdom, with your own eyes—America's dogs are mutts.

Yet every year the nation's professional journalists dutifully inform hundreds of millions of Americans of the "Ten Most Popular Dogs," as determined by the American Kennel Club.

This is of course a grand day for the AKC. Imagine if General Motors published the list of the "Ten Most Popular Cars in America," all ten being of course GM products, and the media faithfully reported it without mentioning, say, Japanese cars. Or Ford's, for that matter.

In fact, mutts are the dominant dog in the United States, accounting for almost 60 percent of all pet canines, according to the Humane Society of the United States. And their numbers are increasing.

The AKC's top ten, based solely on AKC registrations, has recently featured such popular standards as the Labrador Retriever, Rottweiler, Cocker Spaniel, German Shepherd, Poodle, Golden Retriever, Beagle, Dachshund, Shetland Sheepdog, and Chow Chow.

Martin Buser, Alaskan musher and two-time champion of the Iditarod:

"The Ford Model T was at its time the leading automobile, but if we set the standard that that's what all cars have to look like, we'd still be put-putting at thirty miles an hour on the road. Anytime a standard is typecast, development is stifled. It's the same with dogs. A lot of breeds are doomed the moment the American Kennel Club standard is printed, when appearance becomes more important than function, and health and behavior problems set in."

The Ten Most Popular Dogs in America

Here's the true list of the ten most popular dogs in America, according to Rachel Lamb of the Humane Society of the United States.

1. The Brown Dog. The universal mutt type, found from Chicago to Calcutta. He's forty pounds, plus or minus five, short hair, narrow snout, saber tail. A.k.a. Feral Dog, Original Dog, Natural Dog. Sometimes referred to as pariah dog when he doesn't serve humankind. Heaven forbid, he's just being a dog. A dog is a dog is a dog and this, ladies and gentlemen, is a dog. Classically brown but all colors permissible.

2. The Shepherd Mix. Every other stray and shelter dog seems to sport Shepherd angles, Shepherd colors, and Shepherd ears. No wonder. The number of Shepherd mixes in this country outnumbers the number of AKC German Shepherds. Of particular note is the Shepherd-Collie mix, Lassie meets Rin Tin Tin. Even more enduring than their famous parents, this perennial mix has been in reruns for hundreds of years.

3. The Black Dog (frequently, the Black-Lab mix). Round. Hairy. Thirty-five to fifty pounds. Tail sticks out like the small cactus you had in college and never watered. Unimaginably friendly. You

5. The Golden White Dog. A Golden Retriever mixed with a German Shepherd or sometimes a Yellow Lab. A gorgeous, very popular type, gentle with kids, friendly to mail carriers (unless they actually approach the house).

never need a paper towel for spills with this dog around. Every neighborhood has one. Make that six.

4. The Poodle Mix. The curly fuzzy dog. "Oodles of Poodles" is one of the messages NASA keeps radioing to other galaxies to describe our planet. Or so we imagine. Our sun never sets on a Poodle, nine to ninety pounds, in heat. The official standard permits all colors and sizes.

6. Benji-Type Dog. The terrier mix, Brillo hairstyle, comes in any color, six to 160 pounds. Made famous by the brilliant actor and namesake of the group, this mutt is bright, emotional, handsome,

melodramatic, and looks like a mop, sort of like Clark Gable with dreadlocks. Mixing may take some of the fire out of the terrier, but none of the warmth.

7. The Big Bad Fad Dog. Our nation's animal shelters are filled with wide-shouldered, lug-headed, strong-willed, noble dogs. These are the many and mixed offspring of Rottweilers and Akitas, the guard dog fads of the moment. (If she resembles a huge Husky, upper case, think Akita; if she's simply husky, lower case, with Crayola orange facial smudges, think Rotty.) Their looks differ but their hearts are all the same. Begin training classes immediately. If you're one of those folks with more testosterone than sense, a Rotty or Akita mix may be a calmer alternative to the purebred.

8. The Cock-a-Who? The most contrived Cocker mixes are called "Cock-a-Poos," which are so popular some have as many health problems as purebreds, a sure sign of status and demand by the public. For better health, Cocker matches should be made according to the highest principles of Darwinian theory, i.e., love and random mating. The time-honored standard: a long-eared, fuzzy-waggy-happy-yappy dog, smallish size, any color. Can be confused with: Benji-Type.

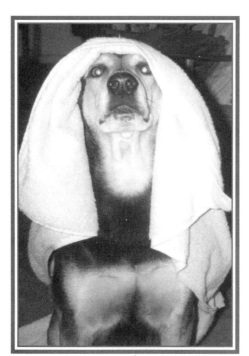

9. The UFO Dog. The Unidentified Furry Object, a.k.a. the Collie mix, though a Collie may have had no part in it. The ubiquitous "Collie mix" may actually have Shetland Sheepdog, Keeshond, Chow, or Samoyed coursing through her veins. Or perhaps a Setter was part of a late-night tryst, or a Soft-Coated Wheaten or the slow-moving Newfoundland from down the street. Regardless of exactly who did what to whom, these delightful dogs come complete with a formal ruff

10. (Tie) Your Dog. Like snow-flakes, every mutt is different. If we've left your incredibly unique and wonderful creature out of this book, please send us a description, with story and photograph, for a future book. Our goal is that no authentic mutt type should go undescribed.

and impressive pantaloons. Every neighborhood has one or two and they all need a good brushing.

10. (Tie) The Sausage Dog. A.k.a. the Hot Dog. These incredibly outgoing sausage-type dogs are easily identified as Basset Hounds or Dachshunds after a few generations of random mating. The slightly taller sausage dog may have Beagle in her—Beagle bloodlines are everywhere—and resemble "Snoopy."

Hybrids Are Like Honda Accords

We understand. Like Oscar Wilde, you want the best of everything. You shelled out $50,000 for a BMW 740, the benchmark of status *and* quality.

Now you want the BMW of dogs.

If you're one of the thousands of Americans who've spent $500 or more on an "AKC-registered dog" from a pet shop or puppy mill or Betty the breeder on the next block, chances are you've blown it, pal. You've bought a Beamer with a Yugo engine.

Sadly, the truth is that popularity in

Einstein and Edison

many AKC-registered breeds has led to temperament problems and genetic diseases. We've bred the Bulldog's head so big and the Chihuahua's pelvis so small most cannot even reproduce by themselves, requiring cesarean deliveries. There are German Shepherds with hips so bad they must crawl upstairs. There's about a 15 percent chance that the Dalmatian riding the fire truck in the Fourth of July parade can't hear the truck's siren because he's deaf. Those are just a few examples.

You can go down the list of the ten most popular American Kennel Club breeds in America, and find many who are victims of overbreeding: Labrador Retriever (cataracts, kidney disease, bladder stones); German Shepherd (in addition to the bad hips, eye abnormalities, cardiovascular defects, and aggression problems); Beagle (epilepsy, heart problems, spinal deformities, skin allergies). American Cocker Spaniels? They not only have floppy ears that get easily infected and have had most of the common sense and purpose bred right out of them; but too many are nasty little dogs who climbed to the top of the biting charts as their popularity soared.

The purebred phenomenon—genetic sloppiness fed by greed—is not true with mutts. Mixed-breed dogs are often healthier, longer-lived, more intelligent, and of more stable temperament. Mixed breeds,

Chelsea

such as the Shepherd-Collie mix, often combine the positive traits of the two purebred lines, such as loyalty and intelligence, while reducing or eliminating the genetic baggage, such as bad hips, aggressiveness, or shyness. This is thanks to the miracle of hybrid vigor.

Hybrid Vigor

We are a nation of immigrants, John Kennedy once said. It is what makes us strong. Well, it's the same with dogs. Geneticists call it hybrid vigor.

"When you breed two inbred lines together, you end up with superior traits with dogs and people," said noted dog geneticist Harris Dunlap. It's no accident that a nation of crazily mixed English, Irish, Italians, Swedes, Poles, Germans, Africans, etc. became the greatest country on earth. Just as it's no accident that dogs crazily bred from mixed Shepherds, retrievers, Huskies, and countless other mutts make the stout beasts who pull Iditarod champions over 1,100 miles of Alaskan tundra each spring.

Hybrid vigor is nature at work. Take, for example, the Natural Dog, or Perfect Dog—Mother Nature's canine ideal. It is a medium-sized mixed breed, twenty to forty pounds, with short- to medium-length hair and straight, erect, normal-sized ears.

This is what dogs were like as the result of evolution—with pelvises large enough to give birth, heads small enough to fit through the birth canal, hair short so it wouldn't be plagued by pests—until humankind started to breed for type, says

veterinarian and author Richard H. Pitcairn. Happily, the Perfect Dog still exists. They come in all colors at your local dog shelter.

All breeds would look something like this, if we flew them all to a Caribbean Canine Club Med for a few years. "Mate a Newfoundland with a Chihuahua, and after ten generations you'll have what looks like a Shepherd mix," said Rachel Lamb of the Humane Society of the United States. "The universal dog—short hair, pointed ears resistant to insects; the basic dog before people started breeding for their own purposes."

Most of what you'll read about mutts—in dog training books and newspaper pet columns—emphasizes their unpredictability and scares the heck out of parents. This simply isn't true.

A study of fatal dog attacks published in 1989 by the *Journal of the American Medical Association* found the great majority of fatal dog attacks were attributed to purebreds.

In 1993, after the latest in an epidemic of purebred Rottweiler attacks led to the death of a sixty-five-year-old South Carolina woman, Randall Lockwood of the Humane Society of the United States, who has a doctorate in animal behavior, declined to recommend specific breeds as nonaggressive. An AKC registration was no assurance, he said, and even dogs believed to be gentle, such as Labradors or other retrievers, have killed people.

Lockwood advised buying spayed or neutered animals, and "mutts, which tend to be less temperamental than purebred dogs."

Adopting an adult mutt from a pound

History, B.C. (Before Collies)

If you're looking for the epochal divide in mutt history, the Great Event separating the periods of B.C. and A.D. (After Dobermans), look no further. It was 3000 B.C.

For an estimated seven thousand years, if Agricultural Man wanted a dog, there was only one kind to get—a dog. Then, in 3000 B.C., the Egyptian Pharaoh Menes I unified Upper and Lower Egypt and began breeding history's first purebreds—Greyhounds, Afghans, and Salukis, who were worshipped as gods. Yet after five hundred centuries of careful breeding, Afghans, according to *The Intelligence of Dogs*, ranked seventy-ninth in a ranking of obedience and working intelligence. Out of seventy-nine breeds.

Yellow Dogs in History

Of all the dog types that conjure the image of "mutt," the Yellow Dog may be the most humble and maligned. Indeed the Yellow Dog has become a symbol of human cowardice, human cruelty, and, as always, canine forgiveness.

Old Yeller, the prototypical Yellow Dog, a yellow Labrador mix, saves his master from a rabid wolf in Fred Gipson's novel and is executed as a potential rabies carrier. The end for this heroic yellow mutt is no happier in the movie version, where Old Yeller saves Tommy Kirk's life and is put down by the boy's pop, Fess Parker.

"Yellow dog has a long history in American slang of denoting a cur," notes William Safire of *The New York Times*, himself continuing the long history in American slang of denoting a cur as something nasty, rather than a lovable mutt. A "yellow dog contract," now illegal, was a labor organizer's derisive term for an agreement signed by a job applicant not to join a union. The term "yellow dog Democrat" was coined in 1928 by Alabamans who remained loyal to the Democratic Party despite their dislike of party presidential candidate Al Smith. "I'd vote for a yellow dog if he ran on the Democratic ticket," the saying went.

Abraham Lincoln had a loyal Yellow Dog named Fido. After becoming president, Lincoln gave Fido to his oldest friend in Springfield, Illinois, John Eddy Roll. Lincoln was assassinated by John Wilkes Booth. Fido was stabbed to death by a drunken man in a psychotic rage.

Perhaps the most spirited defense of the common Yellow Dog comes from O. Henry's short story "Memoirs of a Yellow Dog":

"I was born a yellow pup; date, locality, pedigree and weight unknown. The first thing I can recollect, an old woman had me in a basket at Broadway and Twenty-third trying to sell me. . . . Old Mother Hubbard was boosting me to beat the band as a genuine Pomeranian–Hambletonian–Red-Irish–Cochin–China–Stoke–Pogis fox terrier. . . .

"From a pedigreed yellow pup I grew up to be an anonymous yellow cur looking like a cross between an Angora cat and a box of lemons. But my mistress never tumbled. She thought that the two primeval pups that Noah chased onto the ark were but a collateral branch of my ancestors. It took two policemen to keep her from entering me at the Madison Square Garden for the Siberian bloodhound prize."

often is *more predictable* than bringing home a purebred puppy, he said. "What you see is what you get in temperament." Sometimes they are housebroken. And you're saving a life.

Setting Official Standards

In setting official standards for mutts, we have used the guiding principle that all dogs belong to the same species, *Canis familiaris,* which is Latin for "All dogs are good dogs, it's their owners who sometimes need work." It was all dogs, regardless of breed or type, whom Frederick the Great was referring to when he remarked, "The more I see of men, the better I like my dog." And it was all dogs whom Nietzsche was honoring when he said, "All questions, the totality of all things, can be answered in the dog."

Yes, all dogs come equipped with the remarkable blend of high intelligence, fierce loyalty, humanlike emotions, boundless love, and the ability to smell leftover chicken in an entirely different area code.

It is humankind that has established differences among dogs. Some dogs were selected over centuries for astonishing traits of size and temperament. These dogs were bred for high purposes, such as defending the Roman Empire (the Mastiff), rescuing sailors (the Newfoundland), retrieving ducks (the Chesapeake Bay Retriever), and saving lost mountaineers (the Saint Bernard, later adapted to star in *Beethoven* movies). These are purebred dogs.

To create a purebred, all matters of love are arranged by a *responsible breeder,* whom we prefer to think of as a matchmaker.

Yes, like all the best dog stories, this one too is at heart a love story.

Other dogs—strays, neighborhood dogs, corner dogs, zillions of dogs, most dogs who have ever lived—have met and mated and fallen in love as they saw fit, without matchmakers, lawyers, or prenuptial agreements. This is evident by simply *looking at them.* These are called, simply, "dogs."

Dogs, yes, *all* dogs, are capable of the greatest genetic elasticity among mammals—providing a dazzling rainbow of coat types, head types, tail configurations, and placements. Dogs astonish us with their rich diversity—the 250-pound Mastiff and the five-pound Miniature Poodle are members of the same species, a heart the size of a pecan and a heart as big as a fist both beating with love for us, their best friends. Matchmakers can't perform this trick with cats, horses, or with tomatoes or peas.

In the last century or so, dog matchmakers, carefully molding remarkable lumps of canine clay, have turned out an amazing array of more than 450 distinct breed types, although only 146 breeds and varieties are formally recognized by the American Kennel Club.

Dogs meeting dogs for *entirely unsupervised dates* have done it a little differently. Yappy Yorkies singing a song of seduction to strong, silent Shepherd types. Great Danes falling for Chihuahuas. The results of this dizzying merry-go-round of random matches is nothing less than the richest, maddest,

crazy-quilt variety of mammals of a single species on the planet: mixed-breed dogs.

No wonder the mutt is so beloved! In a world growing every day more uniform, mutts defy all expectations. Soulful Black Labrador eyes sitting low on a Basset Hound body! Amber Golden Retriever ears sticking straight out like furry Cessna wings from the smooth, muscled yellow submarine head of a Yellow Lab. A Collie's delicate noodle nose rising like a thin, airy Museum of Modern Art sculpture on the square block of granite moved from the town center, the stout German Shepherd frame.

Surely there are thousands of types of mixed-breed dogs, roughly familiar, and yet each one unique, like snowflakes.

Yes, this is the entirely foolish ambition of this book: to group snowflakes.

Where to start?

For those of you unfamiliar with *The Complete Dog Book: The Official Publication of the American Kennel Club,* this is the height requirement for the Brittany, the first dog in the book: "HEIGHT—17 1/2 to 20 1/2 inches. . . . Any Brittany measuring under 17 1/2 inches or over 20 1/2 inches shall be disqualified from dog show competition."

Standards for mutts will be relaxed somewhat, and we'd like to reach out right now to all unacceptable twenty-one-inch-high Brittanys. Come home, big fella. We're waiting for you. Only 146 breeds and varieties belong to the American Kennel Club; *all* dogs belong to the family of mutts.

Why pick mutt types? Because most mixed breeds fall into general categories. Because there are four hundred books

you can find if you want to select a pure-bred dog, and not a single guide to mutts. Because the mere existence of purebred standards—and the status purebred implies—has created the misimpression, through no fault of breed owners or fanciers, that *mutts are inferior dogs.* We love purebreds as much as mutts but we'd like to correct this misimpression because (a) it's simply not true and (b) it costs good dogs their lives and good people a full, informed choice every day.

Before the publication of this book, making an intelligent, informed choice—considering fairly the *whole* universe of dogs, including the mixed breeds most people actually own—was never possible.

Now the foolish part. Snowflake groups. Hey, we've got to set *some* rules around here, or it'd be chaos. But they're simple rules. Cross-breeds, or crosses, are the direct product of two distinct breeds, such as the German Shepherd–Black Labrador, and their traits are thus relatively easy to predict.

The remainder of these dogs were described using the sound genetic principle, easily recognized by anyone who already owns a mutt, that when they "look a little like a Labrador" they behave "a little like a Labrador."

These dogs were also classified with careful attention to the high purposes for which they were chosen by their owners, such as retrieving Frisbees and tennis balls, herding children, lap sitting, companion television watching, and cleaning up spilled food products.

We hope you have as much fun with these pages as we did.

Daisy and Texas

What Color Is Your Para-mutt?

The journalist half of the team that produced this book (that's Mike) has a humbling confession: as a nationally syndicated animal columnist and champion of mutts, I am the proud owner of Daisy, a dog. A White Dog. What kind of White Dog I'm not sure. Daisy is Daisy, my beloved dog, her personality and ancestry immutable. For nine years my view of the poor thing has kept changing, like a photograph in a developing tray, while she patiently waits for me to figure out who she is.

It is essential this not happen to you. As a new mutt owner, or longtime mongrel friend, you must solve the mystery, as soon as possible, of who your dog is. Otherwise, you will never know best how to relate to her, or what she is capable of.

It took me almost a decade to realize that Daisy, whom I cast as a guard dog, coulda been a contender as a Frisbee dog. By then, it was too late. She'd lost her vertical leap.

This would be like sending your son to mathematics camp only to realize, after he flunked out of MIT, that in kindergarten he had shown genius at watercolors, and you *just never noticed,* and now he resents you for life. You have to know who your dog is to have a perfect relationship.

Here's how it happened to me. When I adopted Daisy, she was definitely a German Shepherd–Yellow Lab. She had webbed feet (duck dog!), obsessively brought back sticks and tennis balls (retriever!), and her dark eyes smiled out of a sweet blond face (mommy was a Lab!). Mystery solved! Daisy was a Shepherd, of course, because she had a squarish back, pointed nose, and bit the FedEx man twice.

When Brian Kilcommons saw her, he noted immediately the Collie influence in the raised, crimped, forward-on-the-head, antenna-tilted-for-local-broadcast ears. This explains a lot: Daisy's serious, working demeanor in the field; her boss-herding of other dogs; her psycho-obsession with Frisbees, all more like the frantic Border Collie than the sunny Lab.

Now I am quite sure Daisy, my Shepherd-Lab, is mostly a Collie. It took me only nine years to figure this out.

My relationship with Daisy changed completely. Once, I was pained when Daisy failed to be a Lab-like lover-girl who flopped at my feet, knocked against my knees, and followed me from room to room. Now I understand and respect her as she maintains her distance at night, keeping an eye on her flock. Her mom was a Collie! Now I understand her need to chase Frisbees and boss other dogs. We've bonded like never before.

Fortunately, you can compress your own mongrel learning curve to approximately nine minutes, if you read the following Guide to Figuring Out What the Heck Kind of Hound I've Brought Home, developed with Brian and his wife, Sarah Wilson, the well-known dog trainer and author, who has a remarkable eye for these things.

Mary Anne O'Dea

Honey and Cinnamon

PART TWO

101 Mutts

Rusty

Christine Barba

Big brain to learn many tricks.

Beautiful golden hair slightly mussed and outdoors-y.

Intelligent eyes: "Is that my tennis ball you have?"

Strong jaw for picking up everything!

Resting pose, just to prove that they aren't always moving.

Madison

Janet Borraccini Schuler

THE SPORTING MUTTS

The world's greatest all-around family and companion dogs, many random-bred dog fanciers believe, belong to the noble lineage of "sporting mutts." Sporting mutts include some of the most distinguished and popular dog types in America, such as the Black Dog, the White Dog, the Golden White Dog, and the Little Shaggy Dog. (The Black Lab mix, the Yellow Lab mix, the Golden Retriever mix, and the Cocker Spaniel mix, respectively.) The sporting group also boasts other popular mutts, such as the Irish Setter mixes and a mongrelized version of the English Springer Spaniel.

These versatile mixes share many of the traits that make their purebred hunting-dog cousins—such as the Golden Retriever and Labrador Retriever—beloved worldwide. Good, hearty, "real-dog" size (but not so big as to shorten the lifespan). Hale, hey-watcha-doin'-buddy spirits. Gentle souls with hard bodies and life-is-a-hockey-game attitudes. Supreme love of children. A sense of humor; a taste for hard work. (Labrador is Spanish for "farm worker.") And the natural ability to fetch baseballs, tennis balls, Gund bears, and grilled chicken pieces with the gentlest of "soft" mouths.

Long before the nineteenth-century European development of the Lab, Golden, and other bird dogs, all dogs, historians believe, were once sporting mutts, i.e., hunting dogs working alongside their owners. All the popular retriever, setter, and spaniel breeds arose from the best hunting mongrels. This close working bond of human and dog explains the keen intelligence and companionability of our nation's sporting hybrid dogs. Today's sporting mutts also work alongside their owners in the timeless way, hunting for attention.

Descriptions and Standards of the Sporting Mutt

THE RETRIEVER MIXES

The Chesapeake Bay Retriever Mix

The handsome, hardy, American-made Chessie is a Lab with a leather jacket: slightly bigger, more protective, more powerful mentally and physically than the Lab or Golden Retriever. Not as concerned as those two Most Popular dogs about what you, the owner, thinks of his tattoos, T-shirt, and pocketful of Lucky Strikes. Likes the water better than anything. Find one mixed with a softer retriever or a sight hound and you'll be rereading Michener's *Chesapeake* in gratitude.

The Golden Retriever Mix

The ideal purebred Golden is the dog world's 24-karat standard: beautiful, precious, desired by many, worth every penny. The increasingly common flawed specimen, however, can be flighty, nervous, even bitey—in short, fool's gold. A mixed breed often retains more of that golden shine with fewer defects.

The Golden Retriever–German Shepherd Mix

If the gene dice come up sevens, a wonderful combination of the intelligence and loyalty of the German Shepherd with the pleaser and people skills of the Golden. The Golden is a party animal, while the Shepherd, who has already hired the band and set up the bar, is looking at his watch, mumbling, "I've got things to do." A less-ideal gene mix might turn out to be a slightly aggressive, nervous Nellie dog.

The Golden Retriever–Labrador Retriever Mix

The Golden Lab. This is the union of the Mr. and Mrs. Popularity of the dog world. Ken marries Barbie. Extremely trainable, they boast some of the biggest hearts in the canine world. Expect dogs so happy,

Becky Smith

Sadie

loving, and exuberant they're almost goofy. Your retriever mix has an oral fixation—buy plenty of backup slippers for you and yours the first year or two.

The Golden Retriever–Setter Mix

A sublime mix. The loving, athletic Golden merged with the gentle-souled English Setter, mellowing the goofy Golden out just perfectly. If it's an Irish Setter or Gordon Setter mixed with a Golden, beware a beauty-over-brains blend.

The Labrador Retriever Mix

Six tons of love and enthusiasm in a sixty-pound package. Smart, athletic sophomore longing for a guidance counselor. A novice's challenge, a trainer's blessing. Orally fixated. Tremendous drive to retrieve; if not properly focused, may translate into tremendous drive to unstuff the sofa. Sometimes called the Black Dog or the White Dog depending on a Black Lab or Yellow Lab mix. One of the world's great critters, with a little restraint. (Or, failing that, leather restraints.)

The Labrador Retriever–Australian Shepherd Mix

Wow! A young Lab is a runaway boxcar and an Aussie outfits the chassis with Boeing engines. This dog has to have something physical to do—save lives, dominate Frisbee contests—something.

Anything. Repeat often until tired. (Warning: you will tire far sooner than the dog.)

The Labrador Retriever–Chesapeake Bay Retriever Mix

A super dog. Bailey, the Chesapeake-chocolate Labrador in this chapter, is the 1996 Ken-L Ration Dog Hero of the Year. The hail-fellow Lab mixes with the stout Chesapeake like ale and stout to create something wonderful.

The Labrador Retriever–German Shepherd Mix

The Shepherd-Lab. A great all-around dog. Similar to the Golden-Shepherd mix, but potentially a tad less goofy. Goldens tend to be Valley Girls. If they could chew gum, they would. Labs plant their wide feet more firmly on the ground. Labs have a sense of humor, but they're hard workers (with heads shaped to receive hardhats) and combine with Shepherds to make a formidable family dog.

The Labrador Retriever–Sight Hound Mix

A Labrador with a dash of sight hound—such as Greyhound or Afghan—is a charming mix. The hound genes calm down the hyper Lab to introduce a steady, quiet, comfort dog, while the Lab brings a greater interest in people to the who-the-heck-needs-you hound. If you get the Lab atomic energy with the hound desire to run until she drops, well, then you have an Out-of-Sight-Hound. Hybrid vigor can work mysteriously.

THE SETTER MIXES

The English Setter Mix

If your heart is set on a something-plus-setter, set out in search of a harder-to-find English Setter mix. Gentle, loving, smarter, and less hyper than his Irish cousins. A nice mix to call your best friend.

The Gordon Setter Mix

Once, in a kennel we used to manage, there were twelve impressive specimens of the sturdy, handsome Gordon Setter among a hundred other dogs. The twelve

Gordons were the only dogs who had to be shown, every day, how to come in to eat. To eat! Pray that your Gordon mix had his fling with a card-carrying Mensa member, such as a Border Collie.

The Irish Setter Mix

This carrot-topped comely is the gorgeous airhead of the dog world. If the planets are properly aligned, mixed breeding may raise the setter's intelligence level, but expect a dog who is both (a) easily distracted and (b) charmingly absentminded. If you think a and b are the same, the mixed Irish will show you the fine differences.

THE SPANIEL MIXES

The American Cocker Spaniel Mix

Call this, sadly, the American Cock-Eyed Spaniel. Decades of being one of America's favorite purebred dogs have led to many poor specimens being bred. Common Cock-Eyed problems: submissive urination (they pee when you say hello to them), chronic ear woes, and aggression. The miracle of mongrelization may downplay or eliminate these problems, and you'll discover the adorable, loving dog that made Cockers so popular in the first place.

Ira Weissman

Eddie

The English Cocker Spaniel Mix

English Cocker, Sussex Spaniels, Field Spaniels, Irish Water Spaniels, and Clumber Spaniels are five who have been spared the cursed overpopularity and poor breeding of the American Cocker and English Springer. So a Sussex mongrel would make a wonderful dog. But these breeds are rarer, so their crosses are harder to find.

The English Springer Spaniel Mix

See American Cock-Eyed Spaniel, the English's smaller cousin. Sadly, the spring has also sprung on this good-looking, loving dog. Ear and aggression woes too often plague the purebred. However, a Golden Retriever–Springer mix you pull out of the pound may be the world's best dog.

The Spaniel–Labrador Retriever Mix

A charming cross. Slightly scaled down physically and energywise from the Black Lab mix. More likely to sit on the carpet than chew it.

THE POINTER MIXES

The Brittany Mix

The Brittany's mottled white, orange, liver, or roan coat and compact size are signals of a muttlike magic at work. And that's the purebred dog. A true all-around dog, capable of hunting, pointing, retrieving, and loving a family, Brittany mixes are becoming more common as the breed gains popularity. This French fido brings a soft, sweet, athletic, playful, if sometimes shy, nature to any mix. Find one if you can.

The German Pointer Mix

If you're an athlete or hunter, why not fall in love with a German Wirehaired Pointer or German Shorthaired Pointer? These fast, tireless, athletic purebreds are great for finding and pointing at game. But if you're seeking a family dog, look for pointers who have romanced softer types. A Lab-Pointer, for instance, sounds like the stick your chemistry professor used but is a mixed-breed dog worth finding.

The Weimaraner Mix

William Wegman made this rather cold-looking, slightly difficult breed the most photographed dog of the twentieth century. Imagine what you could do with an equally spectacular yet warmer mutt, a Weimaraner crossed with a Mastiff. Mastiff mixes are so big and friendly they tend to be named for states, like Texas, Montana, and Idaho, so call the Weimaraner-Mastiff the Weimar Republic Dog. The wonder of animal shelters is you could walk in the door tomorrow and find a Weimar Republic Dog. The wonder of the universe is life could be found on other planets. Send us a picture if you locate either.

The Blue Dog

Blue Dog Conservative Democrats were those opposed to House Speaker Newt Gingrich. But the most famous Blue Dog, a terrier-spaniel cross, was immortalized by Louisiana artist George Rodrigue, whose paintings of a blue dog with yellow eyes were featured in the Absolut Vodka ad campaign, and sold for as much as $150,000 a painting (collectors include Whoopi Goldberg and Hillary Clinton).

"The dog I paint was my dog for ten years," Rodrigue says. "He died, and I started to paint him as a ghost dog, on his journey to try and find me. I've been painting him now for about seven years. His name was Tiffany."

🐕 The Chocolate Chesapeake Hero

Bailey and Chester Jenkins

McDowell and Piasecki Food Communications, Inc.

Chester Jenkins and his dog, Bailey, were working on the farm that morning near the bull, the two-thousand-pound bull with sharp hooves the size of bowling balls, when it happened.

It was January 1995, a cold morning near Springfield, Missouri. Chester turned his back on the bull for only a second. The bull angrily charged and tossed him ten feet into a watering trough. In an instant the bull was on the farmer, pinning him with his massive weight between the trough and fence, raking his hooves down on Chester's back again and again.

The attack crushed Chester's ribs, broke a shoulder, punctured a lung. He began to bleed internally.

"I knew I was a dead man," Chester said. "Then I saw a blur of brown fur as Bailey charged at the bull." Now it happens that chocolate Labrador Retrievers and Chesapeake Bay Retrievers, the two breeds that form the noble mix that is Bailey, are rugged dogs made to help hunt quarry. Small quarry, like birds.

Bailey, outweighed by a ton, didn't hesitate. He lunged for the bull's head, bit the nose and ears, and hung on despite the bull's efforts to throw him off. Bailey's attack gave Chester, though severely injured, time to squirm under the fence to safety.

Bailey followed his owner out of the pen, then took off for the house to get help. When he wasn't able to alert Iris, Chester's wife, Bailey returned to help Chester into the house. Although he was an outside dog and never allowed indoors, this time Bailey went right inside with Chester. When the paramedics arrived, Bailey ran out to meet them in the yard.

Chester was in the hospital for eleven days. After a long recuperation, he is now fully recovered and back to his farming. Bailey, who miraculously escaped harm, was named the 1996 Ken-L Ration Dog Hero of the Year, receiving a certificate, a commemorative bowl engraved with his name, and a year's supply of dog food.

"Bailey saved my dad," said Chester's son, Dustin. "He's like Lassie or something." Just like Lassie, except Bailey's a mutt. And his story is true.

🐕 The Good Dog Iowa

It was one of the boldest drug-smuggling schemes in U.S. history: a Colombian cargo ship loaded with sixteen tons of cocaine sails into the Port of Miami and unloads $64 million in containerized coke, as safe and unsuspected as sugar.

The supplier was a powerful Colombian cartel accustomed to easy success. In the hold were more than a hundred steel-reinforced concrete posts, legitimate construction materials. Except that every inch of the hollow steel-reinforced pipe was stuffed with cocaine.

Waiting at the Miami port this time stood the federal agent with the most drug seizures in U.S. history. Stood, that is, on all fours, wagging his tail. The dog whose name is legend in U.S. Customs Service lore: Iowa.

A decade ago, German Shepherds were the law enforcement dog of choice. Until the mongrel Iowa, that is, was adopted from a Chicago animal shelter by a drug agent and went on to redefine the standard for drug dogs.

Nowadays most drug dogs are, just like him, the popular and easily recognizable American type known as the Black Dog. "We're looking for a frantic desire to retrieve, incredible friendliness, and great confidence," says Chuck Meaders, chief of the K-9 unit for U.S. Customs in Miami. "These black dogs have the qualities we're looking for."

"We're looking for the dogs in the shelter nobody else wants," adds Iowa's trainer, a U.S. Customs agent in Miami. "Everyone wants a puppy; we want the year-and-a-half-old dog in the pound. Everyone wants the Rottweilers and Golden Retrievers. We want the black dog found in every backyard."

The agent is too afraid of reprisals against him, his family, or his dog to use his name, or photograph, in public. (Smugglers along the Texas border have offered $2,000 rewards for the hides of Customs dogs.) So call him El Papi, the Father. It is his nickname among the drug agents because he loves his dogs like children.

El Papi was there, so proud, when Iowa detected 233 pounds of cocaine concealed in boxes of red roses on a flower flight from Colombia and when a sniff of a suitcase revealed a domino set made of paste cocaine with black-lacquer dots. El Papi spent seven years at Iowa's side, watching the wonder dog make 133 narcotics busts, collar $2.4 *billion* worth of drugs.

"There's a dog in Texas listed in the *Guinness Book of World Records* with several million dollars in busts," says Meaders. "Iowa has that beaten by a wide margin but we're not in the habit of calling Guinness to correct them."

Iowa

U.S. Customs Service

Iowa made one of the biggest drug busts in U.S. history in the time it takes to say, "Sit. Heel. Good dog." When the first container was opened off the cargo ship from Colombia, Iowa started biting and scratching the concrete posts immediately. It took agents five months to remove all the cocaine from the pipes.

How, agents marveled, had the dog smelled the coke through all that concrete and steel? "The bad guys weren't too smart," El Papi chuckles. "Three holes had to be drilled into the side of each post for construction specifications, and they forgot they punched holes in the kilos. For Iowa, it couldn't have been easier."

In August 1992, the day before Hurricane Andrew hit South Florida, Iowa and four other Customs dogs died from temperature extremes in the hold of a plane dispatched to Washington, D.C., to keep them safe from the storm. El Papi wept for weeks. Iowa, eight years old, seven of those years in faithful service to Customs, was about to retire and spend his days playing with El Papi's children, as El Papi's pet.

Not long ago a man disembarking a Boeing 727 from Colombia with a suitcase stuffed with $400,000 in cocaine was astonished to see a very friendly black dog trotting toward him in the Miami airport. It was Homeboy, El Papi's new partner. El Papi was proud, but says it isn't the same.

"My bond with Iowa was so close, and he was an incredible dog, with tremendous capabilities," the agent says. "He was the greatest drug dog of all time. And just an ordinary mutt at that."

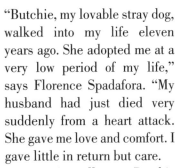 **Butchie**

"Butchie, my lovable stray dog, walked into my life eleven years ago. She adopted me at a very low period of my life," says Florence Spadafora. "My husband had just died very suddenly from a heart attack. She gave me love and comfort. I gave little in return but care.

"I can't really say Butchie has done any great heroic deeds but nevertheless I think she's great. 'Spoiled rotten,' so says my daughter (sibling rivalry of course).

Butchie

Florence Spadafora

"Butchie gives me a big wet kiss in the morning to awaken me. She joins in cocktail hour with decorum and good manners befitting a mutt. She's an enthusiastic companion on our walks and runs, especially when rabbits and squirrels abound. She knows when I'm sad and gives me supportive comfort (big sloppy kisses).

"Butchie is a mutt with a great deal of class. I'm very thankful that I was given the opportunity to be her mistress and companion."

🐕 Lilly, the White Dog

"Lilly was found in a horse pasture when she was about three weeks old," says Leah Plaza of Sun City, California. "We took her to three veterinarians on our way home from northern California. We were told she would not live. She is now fifteen years old and the sweetest, most loving dog. I brought my mother home when she was dying, and Lilly would jump up on her bed and comfort her with lots of kisses. She helped make my mother's last days happy. I have been ill and she comforts me in the same way and is always there for me. She also spends a quiet time sitting with my husband, who has Parkinson's. I feel she is a true gift from above."

Leah Plaza

Lilly

🐕 The Pepsi Retriever

The Pepsi Retriever was nabbed by the dog catcher in downtown Salt Lake City, Utah. Who could have guessed, says her savior, Rebecca Smith, that this common stray possessed superstar skills?

An Australian Shepherd–Black Labrador mix, Sadie has the athletic gifts and never-stop psycho-tude to be an awesome Frisbee dog, and could be a champion if it was anyone's ambition other than hers. "She's always walking around with her Frisbee in her mouth, trying to coax anyone into throwing it," Rebecca says.

Ken Smith cares more about hunting birds. "Sadie outperforms all the purebred dogs who have gone along with them," Rebecca says, "and these are dogs who have had extensive training, unlike Sadie, to be a bird dog. Long after the other dogs are too worn out to continue, Sadie is still bringing back the birds, not only to Ken, but to the owners of all the other dogs."

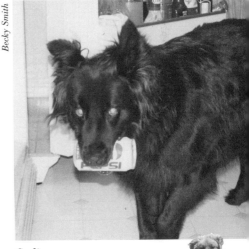

Becky Smith

Sadie

Rebecca, an admitted Pepsi-holic, turned Sadie into a Pepsi Retriever. "Now when I need a drink, I needn't bother getting up from my chair. I call Sadie and ask her to bring me a Pepsi. She runs into the kitchen, pulls the refrigerator door open with a dish towel that hangs from the handle, and runs back with my can of Pepsi. The refrigerator door closes by itself. She has such a soft mouth that the cans don't even have an indentation in them.

"When we have guests over, we'll all be downstairs in our family room and Sadie will make the trip up and down the stairs several times to bring everyone a Pepsi. It took me one afternoon to train her to do this.

"After Sadie, I will never own another purebred. All my future dogs will be from the shelter."

 **The Inedible Journey**

Sandy and Hannah

When the Whites of Washington, D.C., moved to Phoenix, Arizona, Carolyn, Hannah, and the cats flew; Kenneth and the dogs drove. Five days, 2,700 miles. Two dogs and a man in a Honda sedan, crossing the country looking for places to eat.

Restaurants were a problem. Ken is a vegetarian; Ziggy and Sandy are, well, dogs. Ziggy, a Poodle mix, sat on Ken's lap; Sandy, a seventy-pound Golden-Shepherd, sat in the back with her head between the seats, pawing at Ken's arm to try to get Ken to pet him.

"The best place for us was drive-throughs at McDonald's," Ken says. "We'd get a chicken sandwich; I'd take the bread and the shake and give the dogs the chicken. After a while, every time they saw the golden arches they started barking."

Ken was heading to a new job as director of the Arizona Humane Society. At forty-one, he was leaving the smooth power of a Beltway executive job, returning to the daily commotion of running an animal shelter. "I realized I'm more of a hands-on guy and I missed it," he says. "I missed all the characters that in her wildest dreams Flannery O'Connor couldn't have come up with."

He missed the kind of lessons that dogs, not bureaucrats, can teach. He learned the best things from Ziggy, the Maltese-Poodle mix sitting on his lap all the way to Phoenix.

"I've learned through my dogs that sometimes good rules need bending," Ken said.

Ziggy had been turned in to a San Francisco animal shelter when his owner, an elderly woman, was institutionalized after suffering a stroke. Ziggy had spent a terrifying month abandoned in his backyard, matted, filthy, and depressed. No sooner did Ziggy

Courtesy Kenneth White, Arizona Humane Society & the H.S.U.S.

"Butchie gives me a big wet kiss in the morning to awaken me. She joins in cocktail hour with decorum and good manners befitting a mutt. She's an enthusiastic companion on our walks and runs, especially when rabbits and squirrels abound. She knows when I'm sad and gives me supportive comfort (big sloppy kisses).

"Butchie is a mutt with a great deal of class. I'm very thankful that I was given the opportunity to be her mistress and companion."

🐕 Lilly, the White Dog

"Lilly was found in a horse pasture when she was about three weeks old," says Leah Plaza of Sun City, California. "We took her to three veterinarians on our way home from northern California. We were told she would not live. She is now fifteen years old and the sweetest, most loving dog. I brought my mother home when she was dying, and Lilly would jump up on her bed and comfort her with lots of kisses. She helped make my mother's last days happy. I have been ill and she comforts me in the same way and is always there for me. She also spends a quiet time sitting with my husband, who has Parkinson's. I feel she is a true gift from above."

Leah Plaza

Lilly

🐕 The Pepsi Retriever

The Pepsi Retriever was nabbed by the dog catcher in downtown Salt Lake City, Utah. Who could have guessed, says her savior, Rebecca Smith, that this common stray possessed superstar skills?

An Australian Shepherd–Black Labrador mix, Sadie has the athletic gifts and never-stop psycho-tude to be an awesome Frisbee dog, and could be a champion if it was anyone's ambition other than hers. "She's always walking around with her Frisbee in her mouth, trying to coax anyone into throwing it," Rebecca says.

Ken Smith cares more about hunting birds. "Sadie outperforms all the purebred dogs who have gone along with them," Rebecca says, "and these are dogs who have had extensive training, unlike Sadie, to be a bird dog. Long after the other dogs are too worn out to continue, Sadie is still bringing back the birds, not only to Ken, but to the owners of all the other dogs."

Becky Smith

Sadie

Rebecca, an admitted Pepsi-holic, turned Sadie into a Pepsi Retriever. "Now when I need a drink, I needn't bother getting up from my chair. I call Sadie and ask her to bring me a Pepsi. She runs into the kitchen, pulls the refrigerator door open with a dish towel that hangs from the handle, and runs back with my can of Pepsi. The refrigerator door closes by itself. She has such a soft mouth that the cans don't even have an indentation in them.

"When we have guests over, we'll all be downstairs in our family room and Sadie will make the trip up and down the stairs several times to bring everyone a Pepsi. It took me one afternoon to train her to do this.

"After Sadie, I will never own another purebred. All my future dogs will be from the shelter."

Sandy and Hannah

 **The Inedible Journey**

When the Whites of Washington, D.C., moved to Phoenix, Arizona, Carolyn, Hannah, and the cats flew; Kenneth and the dogs drove. Five days, 2,700 miles. Two dogs and a man in a Honda sedan, crossing the country looking for places to eat.

Restaurants were a problem. Ken is a vegetarian; Ziggy and Sandy are, well, dogs. Ziggy, a Poodle mix, sat on Ken's lap; Sandy, a seventy-pound Golden-Shepherd, sat in the back with her head between the seats, pawing at Ken's arm to try to get Ken to pet him.

"The best place for us was drive-throughs at McDonald's," Ken says. "We'd get a chicken sandwich; I'd take the bread and the shake and give the dogs the chicken. After a while, every time they saw the golden arches they started barking."

Ken was heading to a new job as director of the Arizona Humane Society. At forty-one, he was leaving the smooth power of a Beltway executive job, returning to the daily commotion of running an animal shelter. "I realized I'm more of a hands-on guy and I missed it," he says. "I missed all the characters that in her wildest dreams Flannery O'Connor couldn't have come up with."

He missed the kind of lessons that dogs, not bureaucrats, can teach. He learned the best things from Ziggy, the Maltese-Poodle mix sitting on his lap all the way to Phoenix.

"I've learned through my dogs that sometimes good rules need bending," Ken said.

Ziggy had been turned in to a San Francisco animal shelter when his owner, an elderly woman, was institutionalized after suffering a stroke. Ziggy had spent a terrifying month abandoned in his backyard, matted, filthy, and depressed. No sooner did Ziggy arrive at the shelter than an abusive, alcoholic woman burst through the door shouting that her children had been taken away from her and she wanted someone to love. She wanted Ziggy.

The staff, panicking, told her that "the man in charge" had already adopted the little dog. A lie.

The "man in charge" was Kenneth White. Ziggy was dropped on his desk.

"I was not looking for a dog," White remembers. Why, there were important rules against impulse adoptions. They usually ended disastrously. White had *instituted* the rules.

The Whites were, however, thinking about another dog, a big dog. Peaches, their beloved Golden Retriever, had died just months before the birth of their daughter, breaking the family's heart. Ken had never spent five minutes with a dog under sixty pounds. He phoned his wife.

"What do you think, Carolyn, of a small dog?"

"How small?"

"Smaller than the cat."

Uproarious laughter on the line.

"No," she said, "absolutely not."

"Of course I didn't listen to her," Kenneth White says. "I brought Ziggy home."

Ziggy had never eaten dog food, never eaten from a bowl. His teeth were rotten from an addiction to wine and coffee. Now he's "the most wonderful dog," White says. "And our daughter has grown up not sure what species she belongs to. We're a husband, wife, daughter, two cats, and two dogs—a nuclear family of seven."

Sandy, the Golden mix riding in the backseat, came later from a "Free to Good Home" ad. Sandy was aggressive, a cat-chaser, had never eaten anything but hot dogs and bread. A divorcing couple lost interest in her; Kenneth and Carolyn almost gave up on her too. But they stuck by her. Sandy, like Ziggy, teaches her own lessons to folks who get close enough to listen.

"I've learned through my dogs," Kenneth White says, "to respect what Emerson wrote, that a foolish consistency is the hobgoblin of little minds.

"And I've learned that sometimes you have to lead with your heart."

 **Scarface**

On April 12, 1995, a big, happy-go-lucky stray, a Golden Retriever mix, wandered in the path of an automobile in Lantana, Florida, and was struck. As he lay dying, the dog was run over by a second car; the second hit-and-run driver ran tire tracks up the dog's chest.

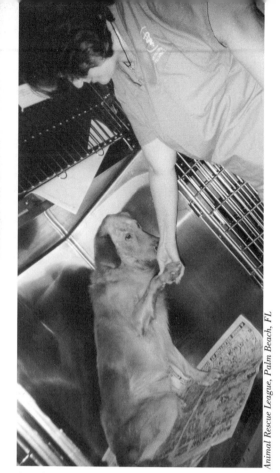

Scarface

Hard as it is to believe, this was one mutt's lucky day.

Thus begins what local folks call "The Legend of Scarface." Minutes later, the police dispatcher radioed George Landon, night ambulance driver for the Animal Rescue League. The Rescue League, supported by animal lovers in wealthy Palm Beach, rises in two hurricane-proof domes designed to seal shut against three-hundred-mile-an-hour winds and to open instantly to the faltering breath of a dog in need.

By the time the pet ambulance driver arrived, Lantana Fire Rescue paramedics had taken time from their nightly rescues of injured people to place a trauma dressing on the dog's head and start an IV.

The stray was in shock, bleeding profusely from the face, with gaping wounds in his head, neck, and abdomen. The skin on his face was flopped open; his right eye hung from its socket. The tire tracks ran down to his abdomen. Rescue League veterinarian Leonid Vidrevich performed two and a half hours of reconstructive facial surgery and stayed up with the dog all night long and into the next day. An X ray revealed multiple pelvic fractures; without orthopedic surgery, which the League was unequipped to perform, the dog would die.

By that morning, the rescue had reached the local TV news and dozens of people wanted to adopt Scarface; others contributed money to a Scarface Fund for additional surgery.

On May 10, a veterinary orthopedic surgeon in Fort Pierce successfully performed the surgery, which cost $1,500, including X rays and a week's stay in the clinic. A month later, after interviewing two hundred people who wanted to adopt Scarface, the Rescue League gave him to Michael King, a twenty-nine-year-old financial analyst, and his wife, Karen Renz, a thirty-year-old law student, of nearby Boca Raton, who already had a purebred female Golden Retriever, Tyler. They changed Scarface's name to Morgan.

"They met all the criteria required for his special needs," said Rescue League executive director Marie Hope.

Indeed.

Michael and Karen use the master bedroom of their two-bedroom condo; Morgan and Tyler have the other bedroom. The dogs have their own toybox with sixty doggie toys.

"We take him to the pet store every Saturday to pick out new toys," Karen says. "We just love him. He's a really sweet dog. After what happened you'd think he wouldn't be. He's just a big baby who likes to jump up on the couch and sit on your lap even though he's huge. He thinks he's a cat—a seventy-three-pound kitten."

🐕 My Darling Clementine

Clementine

A mother was locked in a shed with her newborns, was the word on the street. The makeshift nursery was on the waterfront near the Brooklyn Bridge.

One morning as a man opened the shed to toss some food in, he heard a woman's voice behind him, issuing an order: "I want you to give me the puppies," she said. Over the man's shoulder, in the dirt floor lockup, the woman could see a mother and seven pups blinking in the unfamiliar sun.

"Why don't you buy them from me?" the man countered. The woman gave him all the money she had. "It's not enough," the man snorted. A group of homeless men ambled over, pitching in their last nickels and dimes. "It's not enough," the man repeated.

The homeless men convinced him it better damn well be enough. "Give the woman the puppies!"

That's how Carol Moran and her husband, Michael Galeno, rescued their third dog.

Their second was a surpassingly homely mongrel, pregnant with thirteen puppy embryos, who had been beaten, run over by a car, and left for dead in a trash pile in the East New York section of Brooklyn.

Their first: a wild mutt who jumped on the dinner table, ate the wallboard, and wouldn't take no for an answer from his first family, which gave him up to an animal shelter.

So it was that Carol and Michael, two Brooklyn attorneys in their thirties, launched second careers running a halfway house for

P.S. 19   Angela Morales
Class 5-H   Feb. 7, 1995

Care
Loves people
Eat good food
Must be patien
Extra speacial
Nose works best
Teeth show when snarwling
In a shed and the rescued
Neuter or spayed a dog
Ever so smart.

hybrids without hope. It happens to be *their* house, a nice place with a yard that has gone happily to the dogs.

"Right now we've got a rescued Dalmatian, a purebred that somehow found us, a rescued brindle something, and my husband just picked up an unidentifiable puppy he heard crying, like a child, on Kings Highway. Someone ran over her with a car, crushing her pelvis," Moran said. "And then there's the cat, who's the queen. And our three permanent mutts."

The star of the permanent mutts is Clementine, the wild, wallboard-eating black Spaniel-Labrador mix. He has reformed dramatically, like Shakespeare's Henry the Fifth, into the king of the household mutts.

Carol, an assistant district attorney, takes Clementine into fifth-grade classrooms where the mongrel teaches his ABCs—Approach all dogs with an open heart and respect; Be kind to all animals (the human type too); and Care for animals like you would your brother.

"Our friends say you won't be able to take in any more strays when you have a child," Carol says. "Nonsense.

"My husband says our kid will be the one raised with wolves."

 The Mix and the Perfect Match

Janet Borraccini Schuler found Madison seven years ago when he was a puppy and she was grieving over a dog lost to cancer. "I never thought I'd love another dog as much. Boy was I wrong!"

Madison is "a Golden Retriever–German Shepherd mix, sixty pounds of love," Janet says. He runs in the fields and watches Janet garden. "What makes him so special is he is sensitive and in tune with people's emotions," she says. "By far his best quality is he is so perceptive of when I am sick or in pain.

"You see," Janet says, "I have been living with Crohn's disease over half of my life. When my symptoms flare up and times get hard for me, Madison never leaves my side. He cuddles next to me and lets me know how much he loves me. His soulful eyes show that somehow he understands.

"The last time I was hospitalized, I missed Madison's loyal companionship and understanding ways so much. I knew I was blessed to have him." If Madison was a wonder drug, she thought, how could she not share him?

Madison became a therapy dog. "When I pull into the parking lot of the facility, Madison starts to bark and cry—he can't seem to get inside fast enough. Once inside, he begins to greet people; he knows when to wag his tail wildly and when to be gentle. He never sees wheelchairs, beds, or walkers as an obstacle. He will nuzzle his nose on their lap, or touch their arm just to say, 'I am here just for you today!'

"So you see, not only do I feel Madison is the greatest, but there are so many others who also think the world is a little bit brighter with him around."

Sometimes, Madison gets sick, and it's Janet's turn to comfort him.

"This may not seem so unordinary, except Madison suffers from colitis—the sister disease to Crohn's. Now you see it had to be more than chance that we met. We depend upon each other so much for love and support."

Madison

Janet Borraccini Schuler

Raised tail signals confidence and happiness.

Big nose anything, anytime, anywhere.

Large ears to hear refrigerator door opening from anywhere in the house.

Long legs for taking journeys whenever possible.

Mishievous eyes—if you can catch me you can have my toy.

C.D.

Carol Yowell

THE HOUND MUTTS

Pity the poor, misunderstood hounds. The Afghan Hound is called the dumbest dog on earth by *The Intelligence of Dogs,* which graded him unfairly. The Greyhound is exploited for her marvelous speed and maligned for skittishness, a ridiculous charge. This hound has the Zen calm of the Buddha himself. The Bloodhound is portrayed as a vicious tracker of victimized people; he too couldn't be gentler. The droopy Basset Hound is laughed at as much as with. The Beagle is notorious for her howling. Why, *Webster's Collegiate Dictionary* even defines a hound as "a contemptible person." How unfair.

To understand the hounds, think sight and scent. Sight hounds, like the Afghan and Greyhound, move in brief, astonishing bursts of predatory speed, then hang around the house the rest of the day like Cleopatra, basking in glory. Scent hounds, such as Beagles and Bassets, are more vocal and active, operating on the Nose Knows All principle. Alas, when the nose goes down, the brain turns off.

Marvel, as you read, at what a hound with a little hybrid vigor can do. Elvis Presley's canine muse was "nothin' but a hound dog." Hail now the hound mutts, who have more to offer—somethin' *plus* a hound dog.

Descriptions and Standards of the Hound Mutt

THE SIGHT HOUND MIXES

The Afghan Hound Mix

Despite their intelligence being much maligned, the Afghan Hounds are actually at the top of their class in running miles after deer until the deer drop from exhaustion and the hunters catch up with their bows, arrows, or clubs and begin beating dinner into submission. What? Firearms have been invented? Range Rovers? Swanson frozen macaroni dinners? Nobody told the Afghan. They're stuck in a hunter-gatherer pattern, but an Afghan–Labrador Retriever mix would be a keeper, needing only high coat maintenance and high fences. Once a sight hound mix goes, it's going, going, gone.

The Afghan Hound–Golden Retriever Mix

The Golden Afghan. Lots of hair, sweetness, and speed too. Sky-watchers warning: staring into those beautiful brown eyes could be like trying to make eye contact with the Milky Way. Hello! Is there life on this planet?

The Basenji Mix

The Basenji, an independent, tough-minded African dog, is famous for not having the ability to bark. Ha! Don't confuse this with silence. Your Basenji mix will chortle when happy, yodel when alone, and scream like a crime victim when her will is thwarted. Or wail like a toddler who has heard "No!" Look for a softened Basenji mix—blended with retriever or nice spaniel—and your noisy

Lucky and Gypsy

Shelly Kintisch

barkless Basenji may better listen to your chortles, yodels, and screams.

The Borzoi Mix

The Borzoi dates back to the thirteenth century, to Genghis Khan's hunting parties. She appears to exist in only two dimensions: a giant in side profile, a miniature dog from the front. No width. This dog has to run back and forth in the rain to get wet. Borzois embody the hound dichotomy: sweet comfort seekers at rest, predatory in motion. Not dumb, but scored poorly in SATs because of cultural bias in testing. (See Afghan Hound mix.) Look for a softer, less predatory mix. Don't choose a mix with a terrier, for God's sake.

The Deerhound Mix

In appearance somewhere between a Borzoi mix and an Irish Wolfhound cross, these breathtaking giants of the British Isles look as dramatic as Heathcliff cloaked against the storm. Deerhounds, like any sight hound, can chase small animals, even cats. With training and supervision this is rarely a problem. Any mix probably will be calm, sweet, with a faraway look in his eyes, and a hairdo like he went through the dryer backward.

The Greyhound Mix

With purebred breeding widely influenced by the racing industry, mixes are not easy to find. If you find one in an animal shelter, adopt her! The purebred Greyhound brings breathtaking speed, sweetness, and serenity to any mix or any household.

The Greyhound–Labrador Retriever Mix

A dream union. Amazingly athletic, incredibly sweet, less physical than a Lab (more a Greyhound chariot than a Lab bumper-car). A beautiful creature mentally, physically, and spiritually, unless you're a squirrel.

The Irish Wolfhound Mix

After the Irish Wolfhound exterminated all the wolves in Ireland, no one needed so big and fierce a dog. So breeders transformed it into the sweetest, gentlest, 150-pound fur-covered doorstop imaginable, which he remains today. A wonderful dog who brings no negatives to a mixed marriage except short life. (Therefore, a smaller, longer-lived mix is a fine idea.) The Irish is a Type O dog. Like Type O blood, he works fine with anything he is mixed with.

The Rhodesian Ridgeback Mix

The famous Rhodesian ridge down the middle of the back, like a mountain falling into the sea, often disappears with mixed breeding. This retired lion hunter is a hound mix with the heart of a working dog: large, powerful, very athletic, protective,

Mutts in the Bible

Mutts were a plague upon the ancient Holy Land. So-called pariah dogs, wild critters, scavenged in the streets and spread tapeworm to humans and other animals.

The humble mutt, however, had a defender in Jesus. One day Jesus noticed a horrified crowd backing away from a dead dog.

"The execrable cur was hung for theft!" someone cried.

"He pollutes the earth and air!" said another.

"Detested creature!" cried a third.

But Jesus, like many a mortal who adopts a piebald mutt from the pound, looked kindly upon the common cur. According to an ancient Persian parable, Jesus told his disciples, "Even pearls are dark before the whiteness of his teeth."

with a certain shyness that says, Don't mess with me. Look for ridgeless Rhodesians mixed with more pliable pooches.

The Saluki Mix

"Darling, peel me a grape," says the Saluki. Even more aristocratic than the Whippet, if that's possible. A plaything for the rich, who are always defensively retorting, "No, my dog's not too skinny, she's supposed to look this way." A comfort hound, a jet-sitter. A Greta Garbo hound. Chases only the best rabbits. Chases status, mostly. Brings elegance and aloofness to any mix. Says the Saluki: "You can never be too rich or too thin."

The Whippet Mix

The Whippet is a bundle of blazing speed and charming contradictions: while he can run two hundred yards in twelve seconds, the Whippet at rest is a gorgeous, regal, lamb-sweet objet d'art. His presence enriches a home, like a gray-marble Michelangelo, but he was bred by England's working poor to slay squirrels and rabbits. A Whippet mixed with anything is a lucky find; mixed with an Australian Shepherd or retriever produces a Frisbee champion.

Olivia Goldsmith

Matilda

THE SCENT HOUND MIXES

The Basset Hound–Beagle Mix

This is a little like mixing 1 percent milk and skim milk: they're essentially the same thing. There's little difference in temperament except the Basset Hound prefers an afternoon nap while Beagles are restless problem solvers, charming or annoying depending on the hour. The mix, sometimes called the Bagel Dog, is a world-class beggar, stealer of food, and comfort hound (i.e., sofa dog). If he's a short, knockwurst-shaped dog, think Beagle mix; a longer sausage shape, he's probably a Basset. Both fatten easily, preferring fondu to Fonda as a workout regimen.

The Basset Hound–German Shepherd Mix

A formidable, if funky-looking, dog. A hush-puppy face with a hunter's heart is this hound. Once they set their minds to something—focus being sometimes the problem—hounds can be very persistent. Throw in the Shepherd's high purpose, urgent focus, and strong guardian instinct and pity the rabbits—and robbers.

The Basset Hound–Labrador Retriever Mix

A wonderful mix. A delight to look at and live with. The great all-around Labrador qualities calmed by the Basset's easy personality and sense of humor. Sometimes called the Bassetdor.

The Beagle–Jack Russell Terrier Mix

A Beagle on amphetamines. Where do the batteries go in this thing? All motion, emotion, and mischievous notion. A dog with dreams and the brains to carry them out. Dennis the Menace befriends Bart Simpson. Constant maintenance and supervision required for this model.

Carol Moran, New York attorney and owner of Clementine the Spabador (Spaniel–Labrador mix):

"Hardly any person in the world today is a purebred, it's funny we want it in our dogs. It would seem a true American ought to have a mixed-breed dog, it's the only American thing to do. What comes stumbling up to us in the street and is willing to get in the car invariably turns out to be a wonderful pet."

The Bloodhound Mix

The National Weather Service announces a Major Drool Warning! Mountains of neck folds, mounds of mouth flesh, valleys and rivers forming under pendulous ears. Unless carefully attended to, these natural formations drip and smell, indicating the site of a bacterial Mardi Gras. Mixed breeding eliminates extremes, however. So all the malodorous flesh folds are likely to vanish in a double-helix instant, leaving you with a large love-bucket of a dog. Unless you're a professional tracker or outdoorsman, it'd help if a smaller, more people-pleasing dog had wooed your Bloodhound. Bloodies tend to follow their nose, not you.

The Dachshund Mix

A hound mix that belongs, in spirit, to another class of mutts: the feisty terrier mixes. The Dachshund was created to disappear down little holes and beat up badgers, and for this task is built like a très miniature *Tyrannosaurus rex:* able to rest on her deep chest and still dig with her strong paws. A dash of Dachshund dropped into the mix adds energy, bark, opinion, and the ability to get through the subway gate without a token.

The Foxhound Mix

If you think your dog is an American Foxhound or English Foxhound mix, you've been blowing bugles too long. If you are not a DuPont, chances are you have a Beagle-something. The Foxhound of bugle and hunt is actually a rare breed. As a veterinarian once told us, if you hear hoofbeats in the night, think horse not zebra; if a dog looks houndy, think Beagle not Foxhound.

Denise Boal

Fozzie

🐕 Emily, the Bagel Hound

Ronni Roseman-Hall, a thirty-year-old artist, dreamed of working at the drawing board with a Basset Hound at her feet. She and her husband, Bill, went to the pound looking for a Basset and saw, instead, well . . . *something* low and wide and lop-eared.

"We didn't know what she was, but she had her snout through the cage and was looking really sad and wasn't eating her food," Ronni says. "We left and came back and looked at her again. She was haunting me. It was love at first sight!"

Alas, "I took her home in my car and she proceeded to poop all over it," Ronni remembers. "It took her a long time to get housebroken. She got all the corn out of the garbage and buried one ear in the sofa. She got loose and went to a yard sale. She indoctrinated me into motherhood."

None of that, of course, matters now. Her name is Emily, and she is a beloved Beagle–Basset Hound mix, or Bagel Hound, as Ronni calls her. She inspired Ronni to quit her job taking ads for a small Pennsylvania newspaper.

Ronni was so exasperated going into card shops and finding nothing that even vaguely resembled a Bagel Hound that she launched a business drawing mixed-breed portraits, greeting cards, T-shirts, and so on. "It was all breed-specific. All snotty dogs," she says.

Emily

William H. Hall III

Her clients have included a Bloodhound-Labrador mix and "Poodle mixes, many, many Poodle mixes." She loves her work but, alas, Emily seldom lies at her feet. "Emily has, you know, her day," Ronni says. "Playing out in the yard with Lilibeth, our Beagle, eating everything in the kitchen, and sitting in her spot, looking out the window."

C.D.

 The Story of C.D. (Cur-Dog)

Darlin was a little mutt with a lot of Collie in her who hung around a Florida trucking company until she got hired. The inevitable happened: everyone loved her. "Her only bad habit was stealing brown bag lunches," says Carol Yowell, owner of the company. "Everyone learned to put their lunches up high."

When Darlin died of old age, Carol's husband "was totally upset. For two years he kept saying he wanted a cur-dog—just a little cur-dog. I kept saying no because we were getting ready to retire and we travel a lot.

"Then," Carol says, "the inevitable happened." One of her sons found a ten-week-old puppy frozen on top of a snowbank by a country road in Ohio. One of his legs was damaged so they called him Skippy. When Skippy didn't get along with their other two dogs, they gave him to the Yowells. Skippy got an immediate name change to C.D., short for Cur-Dog.

Truth be told, C.D. did some terrible things not many mutts, or even purebreds, ever do. (And never would have happened had Carol been able to read our mutt training section.) He chewed off the door frame twice, ate lots of pillows and rugs, devoured a beloved pet bird, dropped a possum by their bed at four in the morning. "His first year was puppy time," Carol sighs. No matter. The inevitable had already happened, she says.

"It was love at first sight."

🐕 The Hounds of Bassetdor

One September morning, a California man opened the door of his house and gasped like a Casanova whose trysts had returned to haunt him at last.

There on the doorstep was the equivalent of a strange child crying "Papa!"—a cardboard box filled with seven squirming, squealing black puppies. To the man's horror, the newborns had the face of his unneutered male Black-Labrador-on-the-loose—and the stubby legs and cigar-shaped bodies of Basset Hounds!

In romantic literature, our hearts sing when a Heloise finds an Abelard, when love conquers all differences of history, color, and class, when the pencil-thin man pines over the big-boned woman because their souls are a match.

Alas, the unlikely and completely preventable romance of a noble Lab and a female Basset in Lompoc, California, in the fall of 1992 brought no joy to the hearts of their owners. The offspring were neither proper Labradors nor proper Bassets but, in a favorite word of those who cleave to such standards, "abominations."

Thus, swiftly, the owner of the Basset Hound removed the abominable puppies from their mother when they were one day old, causing the mother to moan with the pain of unsipped milk (and to grieve to an extent for which science has no measure).

Jackson and Clint (Bassetdor)

Patricia Parent

No sooner had the Basset owner dumped the puppies on the Lab's doorstep, than the Lab's owner brought the box to Animal Control, where the foundlings faced certain death.

Patricia Parent, a volunteer at the animal shelter, was stunned, staring at the boxful of one-day-old pups. "How anyone, for whatever reason, could do something this heartless is beyond me," she says. She raged at the irresponsible owners who allowed unneutered animals to breed. Then she frantically worked the phones, calling shelters and vets, searching for a nursing mother. The puppies would die without mother's milk.

No luck.

After the last phone call failed, Patricia decided to bring seven pups home that day to raise them herself.

A veterinarian showed her how to tube-feed the newborns, late at night, early in the morning, worrying like a new mother. Four days later, two of the puppies died, and Patricia wept. The next day, she found a third puppy lifeless and still. "Each time it was devastating for me," Parent says. "I knew there was a good chance I'd lose more of them."

But foundlings, even those outside of Dickens novels, can aspire to happy endings. So it was that the remaining puppies survived and grew up to be "absolutely beautiful dogs," Patricia says.

She kept two, Clint and Jackson, and found homes for the others. Sometimes all four Bassetdors, as a local veterinarian calls them, get together for a family reunion. Anyone who sees them has to laugh, or, if that person is having a terribly bad day, at least force a smile. That is the gift of the hounds called Bassetdors.

Kenneth White, director of the Arizona Human Society:

"I love the Golden and Lab temperaments. But what we're seeing in those breeds right now because of inbreeding is a lot of aggression. It's really sad to see a Golden growling and a fear-biting Lab. And we're seeing them in these wonderful dogs. Get a Golden or Lab mix and you'll probably be better off."

🐕 Bruno Brown

It was just after dawn in southern Indiana, a spring morning. Bruno Brown, farm dog, was making the rounds of his nineteen acres, scaring up rabbits. "He likes to check out the rabbits," says farmer Lewis Brown, Bruno's owner. "Although he never catches any."

Bruno is a slow little submarine dog, a mini–German Shepherd on Basset Hound legs. Been on the farm since he was a pup. Now he's eleven, sleeping more, stayin' out of the way. But on the morning of April 29, 1993, Bruno saw a scene that disturbed him.

A truck wandered onto the road on Bruno's land and got stuck in the mud, scaring away rabbits. Out stepped a bear of a man, six foot seven, over three hundred pounds, and a woman who looked afraid. The man was carrying a knife. He was forcing the woman toward Bruno's woods.

Bruno assessed the scene and attacked. "Went right for his throat," Lewis Brown said later, "allowing her to get free and run to a nearby residence where she called police." The woman said later she thought she'd be raped and "that dog probably saved my life."

Lewis Brown was surprised himself. "That was a pretty big load for a dog like Bruno. He's not a real big dog, and for the most part he's pretty gentle. I don't know what got into him. I suspect he thought it was one of my daughters who was being attacked. He gets real upset about violence. Doesn't like it, even when the kids are playing around."

Bruno Brown was honored on the steps of Owen County Courthouse, and driven all the way to Indianapolis to meet the mayor, Stephen Goldsmith, who gave him a biscuit. Today Bruno is back on the farm, rising early to greet the day, not botherin' anyone but rabbits.

🐕 Mama and Babie

When the hurricane stopped in Miami right on schedule like a freight train derailing, Mama huddled in the dark in her small concrete house with two candles, a book, and her Babie.

Mama is Norma Davis, seventy-one, grandmother, widow, retired Western Union clerk who'll tell you she's seen plenty of big ol' hurricanes (Andrew, Donna, Betsy) and plenty of sweet little hybrid dogs (the late Boy Dog, Mandy, BB, and Bonnie, to name a few).

"I knew Andrew was gettin' big at three in the morning when I heard a *bonk* and the oak fell on the corner of the house," Norma says. "I've been in this house through forty-five years of hurricanes, and a lot of memories. But I just petted Babie and loved her and told her everything'd be okay, and it was."

This is how Mama got her Babie, the sweetest mutt of all:

"Tommy Davis, my second husband bless his heart, was a sweet lil' ol' Georgia cracker and he loved dogs. He also loved all that ol' Georgia cookin', fried okra, chili,

the best barbecue you ever did see, T-bone steaks, a pack and a half of Camels a day, a six-pack of beer a day at least. He was a skinny little guy, but he worked hard as a nurseryman and he could put it all away."

When Tommy lost a leg above the knee from hardening of the arteries, he and Bonnie, their Collie mix, would watch TV. "He'd lie in bed and Bonnie would get up and back to where the stump was and keep his leg warm, stay right there with him all day watching TV, go out the dog door to the bathroom, get right back on his leg," Norma remembers. "Tommy would say, 'She's the best nurse I ever had.'"

Mama and Babie

Tommy died at home, at age seventy. When the doctor left, Bonnie jumped up on the bed, "smelled him slowly from head to toe, then she laid down next to him and washed his head," Norma says.

When Bonnie died seven years later, Norma grieved for six weeks. Then, in May 1992, "I went over to Bonnie's vet and cried my eyes out. Suzie, the receptionist, says Norma stick around. Another woman is coming in with a Lab mix. You might like this little one. Sure enough I stood out there when she drove up. Babie was an independent little thing, but absolutely stunning.

"The next day, she was recovering from her anesthesia after being spayed and I went in and looked down at her lying there all groggy barely able to open her eyes and I said, 'You wanna come home with me?' And all of a sudden the tip of her tail started coming up and down. And I said, 'Well, good. I'm taking you home.'

"The first night I was in bed and I didn't know where she was. I found Babie curled up in a dark corner of the kitchen. I said, Babie, I didn't bring you home to sleep in the kitchen. I brought you home to sleep with me. I carried her and put her on a corner of the waterbed and she stayed the night.

"She lies around here as pretty and aloof as Queen Nefertiti. At five in the morning she gets in the waterbed with me, rolls on her back, and says, Well, if you're going to kiss me, kiss me now. I kiss her and nuzzle her like crazy and once in a while she will reward me with one lick on my cheek.

"When I go outside people say, 'My, what kind of dog is that?' I tell them, 'good question. It's a one-hundred-percent Waterbed Dog. And she's my Babie.'"

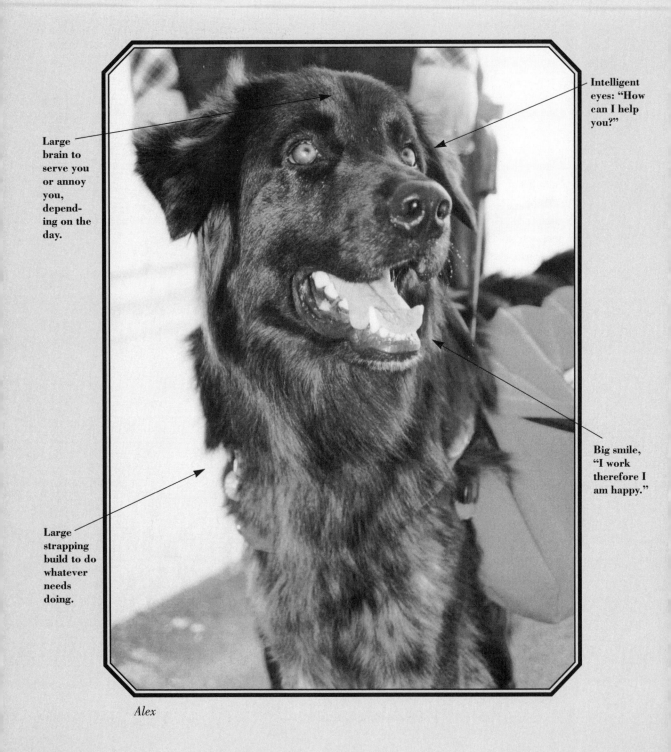

Intelligent eyes: "How can I help you?"

Large brain to serve you or annoy you, depending on the day.

Big smile, "I work therefore I am happy."

Large strapping build to do whatever needs doing.

Alex

THE WORKING MUTTS

Working mutts are some of the most massive, strong, brave, and awesome creatures we, as Homo sapiens, can count as true friends.

Nietzsche once said, "The world was conquered through the understanding of dogs; the world exists through the understanding of dogs." This makes sense only through the understanding of working mutts, who were the first dogs to befriend humankind, fourteen thousand years ago in Israel; who conquered the wilderness and nature, red in tooth and claw, in service of humanfolk; who held the lion, bear, and wolf away from our food sources and our children; who marched in phalanx to take and retake the continents (the biggest mutts were molded into the Mastiff, the M-1 Tank of ancient armies).

Today's hardworking mutts include the most imposing guard dogs sniffing the four winds, spawns of Akitas, Rottweilers, Mastiffs, Bullmastiffs, Great Danes. The hardy Alaskan Husky superhybrids who conquer the thousand-mile Iditarod trail, leaving purebred dogs in the snowdust. Gentle giant mixed Dane service dogs to the blind and disabled. And mixes of Saint Bernards and Newfoundlands, those gentle lifesaving giants of snow and sea.

Descriptions and Standards of the Working Mutt

THE FLOCK-GUARDING MIXES

The Great Pyrenees Mix

If you're looking for a snowdrift of a dog, the Pyrenees mix is the one to adopt, the one who usually loves children and doesn't bite people. Pyr (pronounced "peer") mixes can be adopted at the animal shelter, and are the sweetest dogs among the livestock guardians. Three thousand years ago, Pyrs wore spiked iron collars to protect themselves while fighting wolves, but breeders have subsequently softened them into gentle family dogs with formidable guard dog instincts intact. If you don't mind size and hair, this big, hulking, white hunk of a dog would be a nice addition to almost any mix.

The Great Pyrenees–Alaskan Malamute Mix

The Great Pyramute. A big, white drop-dead beauty with easy charm. Malamutes are always grinning and have an outrageous sense of humor; Pyrs are laid-back guardians. This mix is happy to do her own thing and hang out with you too. Owners wonder, "Why is this dog always smiling?"

The Moby Dick Dog

Giant, white, gorgeous, epic creatures, formed from centuries of the bravest and most aggressive mutts, they could turn you into Ahab and your life into a mythic struggle should you take one in. Every now and then innocent dog lovers make this mistake: they see in a dog book a picture of an absolutely magnificent white creature on the retriever model, twice as big. The Kuvasz and Komondor of Hungary. The Maremma of Italy. The Anatolian Sheepdog of Turkey. And they want one. A mix of any of these whales would likely be a guard dog of unrivaled assertiveness, as gorgeous as a polar bear and equally fierce when aroused. You don't want a Moby Dick mix unless you have livestock to protect. With one exception: see Great Pyrenees mix.

THE GENTLE GIANT MIXES

The Bernese Mountain Dog–Golden Retriever Mix

A splendiferous mutt. Big, friendly, sweet. You practically need an insulin shot to own one.

Casey

M. P. Knecht

THE TOMB OF THE UNKNOWN MUTTS

Mutts are history's forgotten army. Reading histories of dogs at war, one imagines the primary mutt contribution was to dodge the draft. For thousands of years, mixed breeds served their countries by watching the women and children while purebred dogs went to war.

During World War II many mutts served America as sentries, messengers, airplane spotters, pack carriers, "and other tasks which must remain secret" (official government language), but in most wars breeds get all the credit. Soldiers and war chroniclers too often can't identify mutt types, which is why we wrote this book. (War chronicler to soldier: "What kind of dog is that on the front line, dodging bullets?" Soldier: "That, my boy, is a German Shepherd." Chronicler: "And who's next to him, pulling that injured private to safety." Soldier: "That, my boy, is a Brown Dog.")

Many breeds were indeed called to serve for specific traits—the bravery of the Irish Terrier in World War I, the all-around skills of the German Shepherd in World War II, the size and ferocity of the Mastiff in ancient armies. But since Mastiff means, technically, very large fighting dog with heavy head, we're confident there were a few of mixed blood among the eight thousand mastiffs in spiked collars and full suits of mail that Queen Elizabeth used to suppress an Irish rebellion in 1560; that a few mixes from doggie one-night stands served as Mastiff "Biters of the Enemy" for the Assyrians 300 years B.C. And so on.

A monument honoring American canine war dead is being erected in Washington, D.C. Next to it should stand, or rather sit, the tomb of the unknown mutt.

The Great Dane–German Shepherd Mix

A wonderful dog. The Dane adds size, sweetness, and calm to the athletic, alert Shepherd, but the Dane too can be a serious guardian when aroused. A great mutt to meet as a friend, not as a stranger or, Allah help you, an enemy.

The Newfoundland–Labrador Retriever Mix

As sweet as a Jamaican cargo ship of sugarcane and almost as big. The Lab blood energizes the Newf, awakening the giant. Still a relatively laid-back, people-loving, water-loving, hair-shedding, ball-chasing, child-slobbering love puppy.

The Saint Bernard Mix

Alas, this lifesaving, legendary breed has been overbred. The canonized canine is now something of a loose cannon. Sometimes he's trustworthy and sweet; occasionally he makes you nervous passing him on the sidewalk. Beware Saints mixed with other big, aggressive breeds. Then the Saint (Saint Elsewhere) is replaced by the devil. A softer Bernard mix, though, may be a true candidate for having his own day of veneration.

The Saint Bernard–Golden Retriever Mix

The Golden Saint, with qualities that justify the name. "Dreyfuss" on *Empty Nest* is a Golden Saint, one-hundred-pounds-plus with long red hair and huge black-masked face. At her best, a Golden Saint is a huggable sweet giant who doesn't drown you in drool. Careful: both these breeds tend toward terrible hips. Like your favorite aunt, the Golden Saint may have a wonderful heart and bad hips.

THE NORDIC MIXES

The Alaskan Husky Mix

This wildly mixed supermutt is the only dog in the world who can consistently endure the 1,159-mile ice-and-snow iron-dog competition called the Iditarod. He does more than hold up; he *likes* it. The poster pooch for hybrid vigor. Great if you're a musher, but if you inhabit the Lower Forty-eight an Alaskan Husky is a less practical choice unless your idea of fun is spending a rainy weekend at home with a subverbal triathelete.

The Samoyed Mix

Like most Nordics, this pretty white creature grins like a fool, but hardly is one. Great sense of humor, family-oriented. Sammys are the essential role-players of the dog world: like a good sixth man on a basketball team, they're not great at anything but good at almost everything and

you can't do without them. Like tapioca, a Sammy softens and sweetens the dogs it romances and mixes with.

The Samoyed–Labrador Retriever Mix

The Some-More-Lab. Says after eating, "Please may I have some more." This mix can inherit the Lab tendency to get fat. That famous oral fixation gets focused, not as the Earl of Malmesbury intended when he founded the breed, on Fig Newtons. This mix is probably calmer and less physical than a Lab, in fact, but a useful all-around companion. Dead ringer for a Collie-Shepherd.

The Siberian Husky Mix

If you're seeking a scent of the Klondike, the Siberian Husky mix is a sound choice. In purebred form this grinning, happy breed can fool you, turning independent and somewhat predatory. Tough, aloof, made to run forever, they need a fence and training to become the ideal family dog. Hybridization, however, can make the Siberian better by half. (A retriever or hound may be the better half.)

THE PROPERTY- AND PEOPLE-GUARDING MIXES

The Akita Mix

Hair, you gotta love it. Akitas shed once a year—for 365 days. Hybridization with a hound or other friendly-passive type can soften the essential Akita, who is aggressive, aloof, and needs lots of training and socialization.

The Doberman Pinscher Mix

The fearsome-looking Doberman Pinscher, the scary dog of grandma's generation, has been recast by breeders into a sweet-as-molasses weather-wimp with stunning athleticism and beauty. A Dobie-Retriever mix would be a prize indeed, and is probably available at your local shelter.

The Mastiff–German Shepherd Mix

Mastiffs are bearlike giants and their mixes are big, lovable lugs. The label on the Mastiff mixing bottle says: These ingredients add size and inertness. The offensive tackles of the dog world. Off the field they kick back and crack a beer. Just how big and how lovable depends on the mix. A Mastiff-Shepherd can be sweet as marmalade, reach 150 pounds, and yet run with retrievers, a far more athletic beast than the purebred Mastiff.

The Mastiff-Rottweiler Mix

A two-hundred-pound English Mastiff combined with a 130-pound Rottweiler is an awesome creature of great use on farms, as a conversation stopper, or a slow-moving piece of furniture. Must be

Private Chips

The U.S. Army's official mascot in World War II was a German Shepherd; the Marine mascot was a Doberman. Of all the 25,000 dogs drafted into combat by the United States, the most decorated war dog was a mutt named Chips, a Collie–Husky–German Shepherd mix. Private Chips earned his, uh, stripes and spots performing heroics during the invasion of Sicily, during which he captured a machine-gun nest and was wounded. Chips was awarded the Silver Star but, alas, was denied the Purple Heart. We don't know if Private Chips was bitter. We do know that after the war he had a chance to meet General Dwight D. Eisenhower and bit him.

Texas

under verbal human control at all times. Toby, a Mastiff-Rotty we know, is an incredibly sweet double-wide Rotty with a U-Haul for a head. Toby can plow through most man-made barriers, is smart enough to open the latch on most gates, and seems to have a definite agenda that doesn't include people, Lord help us all.

The Rottweiler–German Shepherd Mix

Overpopularity has hurt these two breeds, but together they can make a wonderful pet, albeit one who needs lots of training and socialization. A formidable dog, devoted to hearth and home. Smart and protective.

The Rottweiler–Ridgeback–Pit Bull–Boxer Mix

The R2B2. Yowch! (A hybrid of Wow! and Ouch!) Every breed in this combination adds energy, intelligence, and what the R2B2's loving mother calls "intensity." An extremely smart, devoted, high-powered mutt. Read the small print on this concoction: Warning. Contents under pressure.

🐕 Boots: The R2B2 Hound,
or
The Dog Who Came up by His Bootstraps

Her father was a farmer from Genoa, Italy, who saw animals as animals. Until the night the family mutt, Gina, died, and he wept over the body.

In the way generations improve on each other, Lina Striglia, thirty, is a farmer's daughter who volunteered at the SPCA in Northampton County, Pennsylvania. The first week, Lina's eyes swelled shut from cat allergies. Luckily, Lina's eyes got better just in time to volunteer the next week. She kept coming, week after week.

Sometimes folks marry people a bit like their parents. So it was that Lina's husband, Sam, a computer consultant, had two rules: no crying over homeless animals, no bringing any animals home as pets.

"Of course," Lina says, "I was unable to follow either rule." On the night before Lina and Sam were to leave for a week-long vacation, Lina saw "the cutest, sweetest Boxer, Pit Bull, Rottweiler, Ridgeback mix ever."

Boots, a stray, "spotted me at the same time and it was truly love at first sight," Lina said. "He cried when he saw me minding other dogs at the shelter." On vacation, Lina couldn't shake the memory of Boots—and spent the week trying to convince everyone she met to adopt him.

When vacation was over, "Naturally, I assumed he'd be gone—the cute puppies usually don't last long." But Boots was still there! Said Lina: "I brought him home, much to my husband's dismay."

Boots

Lina Striglia

One of Sam's rules had been broken. Sam was upset.

Upset, that is, until the man and the dog got a good look at each other.

"Sam and Boots fell in love the moment they met," Lina says, "and have been buddies ever since."

🐕 Susan and Joe

Susan, a nurse, is five feet tall, 100 pounds. Joe, a Great Dane–German Shepherd, is a head taller, 105 pounds. When they met, at the dog pound in Seattle, he was four years old, unneutered, "barking at everything, the attention span of a flea," Susan Duncan recalls. "Typical testosterone poisoning." But she was charmed. The big goof put his paws up on her shoulders, looked down at her like a big brother, knocked her over. Susan was weak that day, couldn't get up. The multiple sclerosis was bad. So Joe picked her up. Practically carried her to the car. Joe and Susan, Susan and Joe. Theirs was an animal shelter match made in heaven.

Caitlin Hickey

Susan and Joe

Within minutes after their first meeting, they moved in together.

Joe works the ATM machine, does the laundry, opens the refrigerator door, fetches eggs. Susan says, "'No, Joe. We don't need the milk!' It's so heavy he has to bite the carton hard and we get milk fountain!"

Susan Duncan, thirty-eight, was afflicted at nineteen with MS, a disease that short-circuits the nervous system's signals to the brain. Its cure remains a mystery. Joe, eight, was gifted at birth with that canine need to help and love human beings.

Susan can't get out of bed without Joe. "In the morning when I open my eyes Joe is there to take the covers off. Heat worsens the disease and it's good to cool off. Joe pulls off the comforter and pulls my feet out of bed, grabbing my toes, swinging me gently out of bed. He's got a soft mouth. He brings me my cane in his mouth and I stand and get my balance."

Leaving the house is impossible without Joe. "He normalizes my gait, keeps my balance. Before Joe, if I fell down, I'd have to wait for someone to find me. Now if I fall down, he lies next to me and pushes me up so I can assume an upright position. I'd be in a wheelchair without him."

In the city, Joe pushes open the doors of office buildings for Susan, helps her find her car when she forgets where she parked it, acts as a guide dog when her vision goes bad, locates bathrooms.

"What I find remarkable is he has never taken me to the men's room," Susan says.

At ATM machines, "My fingers are so numb, I can't grip the money and it blows all over the parking lot. One time a young boy took my money and ran. Now Joe gets the money out of the slot and the receipt and gets the card out of the slot for me. No one takes money away from Joe."

Susan, however, won't give her companion her PIN number. "He'd clean me out," she laughs, "buy out the dog biscuits, head for Mexico. He can open the front door, open the car door. It'd be the last I'd see of Joe."

🐕 Chops

One night in New York City, a young man adrift on the sea of life left a Burmese restaurant and found his fate on a lamppost: FREE PUPPIES! GOLDEN RETRIEVERS PLUS BURMESE MOUNTAIN DOGS.

The future opened to Ross Becker like a fortune cookie crumbling. He'd always wanted a Golden. What a Burmese Mountain Dog was he hadn't a clue, but had he not just eaten a Burmese meal? Anyone could see the pawprint of destiny at work. So he called. The folks were artists, said come on over. Whereupon Ross was surprised to find there were no Golden Retrievers to be had. And no Asian mountain dogs, either. Just some sort of smooshed-palate pups. "Goldens and Burmeses all mixed together in large, furry black puppies."

The next night, at a Chinese restaurant, Becker and his wife named their mystery pup Chops (full given name, Chopstick), in honor of her Asian heritage.

"It was only later we discovered Chops was a *Bernese* Mountain Dog, from Bern, Switzerland, not a *Burmese* Mountain Dog, which doesn't exist," Becker says. "Obviously I didn't know much about dogs."

In all good dog stories there is a catharsis, and in this one the dog inspired the man to study hard and learn something about dogs. Today Ross is publisher of *Good Dog!*, a consumer newsletter for dog owners.

Chops

Chops has arguably the best job in the canine world—columnist and senior test dog.

A seventy-seven-pound Golden Retriever, except for the fact she is too big, and the wrong color (all black, one of the three colors of the Bernese Mountain Dog), Chops is no prima donna columnist. She works the copy machine in the magazine offices in Austin, Texas.

"The command is 'Go copy,' and she stands up and presses the copy button," Becker says. "The problem is, her paws are so big she invariably presses ninety-nine copies when all I want is one."

Chops retrieves and distributes faxes. She picks up scraps of paper off the floor, receiving a treat for tidying up. (When the floor is perfectly clean she pulls paper out of the wastebasket and presents it for treats.)

All the wonders of the canine consumer world are brought before Chops for appraisal. Chops sleeps on cedar beds with faux down comforters, hangs out on Hound Loungers, is splashed with jasmine perfume for dogs from French crystal bottles. But Chops is a down-to-earth girl. "She likes my bed best," Becker says. "And her favorite scent is dead animal. She loves to roll around in it to get the perfume."

As for treats, Chops likes pasta for dogs, Pet Pupcorn, Bowser Brittle, and Nookies Cookies.

"The trouble with Chops as a test dog for treats," Becker admits, "is she likes everything."

In her column, Chops routinely defends the rights of mixes and orphans like herself. "Chops likes to say we at the magazine don't discriminate against any dog on the basis of race, creed, color, or mysterious origin," Becker notes.

"We call her a Cajun Dog, or Blackened Golden," Becker adds proudly. "She's an excellent example of the breed."

 A Dog's Love

Some believe the love between human and dog is idyllic; that dogs, who were not expelled from Eden, can show people the gift of paradise. Others put great store in the fact that dog is God spelled backward.

Don Kretzschmar, fifty-two, Lutheran pastor, modern shepherd on the flatlands of northern Illinois, chaplain for six institutions for the mentally handicapped, husband, father of two teenage daughters, owner of Mieshka, a huge Great Pyrenees mix, hasn't time for such questions.

To the pastor, a dog's love is a simpler matter. In the Bible, the pastor says, is this story Jesus told: Once there was a rich man who lived lavishly. Lazarus, one of many so-named in the good book, was a scabrous beggar, leprous, sore-pocked, who pleaded for crumbs at the rich man's house. He was refused, shunned.

"Here is a man who is rejected by virtually all people," Pastor Kretzschmar says, "and the mongrels of the street come and minister to him, lick his sores."

In an institution near Wheaton, Illinois, there is a severely mentally retarded woman named Laura. Laura, in her late twenties, "sits rocking back and forth in autistic fashion and has never been known to utter a word," the pastor says. "When approached, she clasps her torso and shakes her head, refuses to use her walker or participate, pushes away, shuts out the world."

When Mieshka, seventy-five pounds, not a licker, not a tail-wagger, moves slowly, steadily, to Laura's side, "Laura stops her rocking and her face lights up in a smile like you seldom see," the pastor says. "Then she reaches out to pet and embrace Mieshka. There is this warmth and joy they share in being together. It's delightful.

Mieshka

Don Kretzschmar

"We all need relationships that have both simplicity and mystery," the pastor says. "Mieshka and I don't claim to comprehend each other, but we know we can trust our friendship. I think there are qualities like that in my relationships with the people I serve. I am their friend. To be a true friend does not require comparable intelligence or capability."

🐕 Martin Buser and D-2

As Martin Buser mushed his sled dogs along the Iditarod Trail, now and again he would stop, open a small sack, and scatter his father's ashes onto the snow.

Buser's father, Peter, died at seventy-one in 1994 in Switzerland, without ever visiting Alaska, where his son arrived penniless fifteen years ago, with nothing but a backpack and blue jeans, and established a dog sled dynasty. Without ever seeing his son win the world's greatest sled dog race twice, in 1992 and 1994, setting new records both times.

Leading Buser's team is the legendary Alaskan husky named D-2—a mutt. It's a myth that Iditarod dogs are Siberian Huskies, a pure breed. In fact almost all Iditarod racers are Alaskan Huskies, a wildly mixed-up breed. "Hybrid dogs are the best," Buser says. "These are the greatest of mixed-breed dogs."

The official standard for an Iditarod dog, he says, is "anything that pulls hard and likes to run."

D-2

Buser has finished in the top ten eight times with teams of Alaskan hybrids; in 1980 and 1981, his first two years, he raced a team of purebred Siberian Huskies and "did about as well as anyone ever did with them. The best I did was nineteenth."

Siberian Huskies "are just not totally competitive, not as gutsy as my guys," Buser says. "They always keep their reserve tank full. My dogs are incredibly driven; they literally want to race all the time. Siberians like to take it easier."

Rick Swenson, five-time winner of the Iditarod, agrees. "We all use mutts, no one uses *breeds*," he says, spitting out the word. "I've got a lot of Border Collie in my dogs because they love to run, are smart, and have great heart. Also Cocker Spaniel, Saluki, gazehound, Belgian Sheepdog, German Short-Haired Pointer. I know guys who mix in Coonhounds, bird dogs, Golden Retrievers, Labs . . . It's so mixed up, no one knows what's in the dogs. Any dog that loves to run can do it, and mutts have more heart."

D-2 "gets high on being a competitive athlete," Buser says. "He never gives up." D-2, who hails from a long line of Alaskan sled dogs mixed with setters and Lord knows what, was honoring his own father on the trail in 1995. "D-2 is short for Dagger the Second," Buser says with a smile. "His old man, Dagger, is still around.

"My dad, I took him on the Iditarod, one way or another."

🐕 The Vendor

Evelyn Roper, hot dog vendor, took a bus home from her job to the depot in Camden, New Jersey. Across from the transit building she saw a forlorn, frightened puppy begging for food from folks waiting for the bus.

Evelyn offered the pup one of her hot dogs. He took it, hid under a bench and ate it. Coming closer for a second hot dog, the puppy appeared mangy and smelled very bad. "This did not detract from his cuteness," Evelyn remembers. "He was a mix of Shepherd and who can tell what else." As he ate, "I placed my scarf on the ground so the poor little thing would have something between him and the concrete," she recalls.

Right about then, Evelyn's husband, Trey, arrived to pick her up. "Do you see my scarf?" she asked. He responded: "Do you want to take him home?" Evelyn was going on about already having three cats, a rabbit, four fish, a turtle, two preschoolers, and no yard of any size as Trey opened the car door and called to the puppy. Tuffy, his name to be, clambered over Trey, over the back seat, and sat next to four-year-old Traci.

"Oh, Mommy, look!" Traci cried. "I've got a puppy." And so it was.

Traci and Tuffy

Evelyn Roper

Supris-
ingly big
teeth,
just in
case.

Albert Ein-
stein hair.
The scruf-
fy chic.

Clint East-
wood's
eyes: "Go
ahead,
make my
day."

Heart of
a lion.

Beard to
collect
food with—
you never
know when
you'll want
a snack.

Strong
feet and
nails for
digging
big
holes.

Judy Davis

Gladys

THE TERRIER MUTTS

The terrier mix is everyone's mongrel. She is uncommonly brave, spirited, smart, and loyal, affordable to keep, and econo-sized to boot. It's no accident that a terrier mutt, a pound dog, became the most beloved dog in the world: Benji. If you haven't seen at least one *Benji* movie, please take a five-minute stroll outside before reading further. You will see a Benji-Type.

Before Benji and Fala, FDR's Scottish Terrier, the terrier and terrier mixes got hardly any press. Legendary were the deeds of the sporting dogs of Egyptian pharaohs, Viking chieftains, and European kings, huge canine hunters of bear and boar. Nothing was written of the scrappy little peasants' farm dogs who went to *terra*, Latin for earth, to slay fox, badgers, and rats.

When you adopt a terrier mutt, you will not be getting a pure authentic terrier type. Luckily for you. The absurdly courageous purebred Irish Terrier, no more than twenty-five pounds, has been reported refusing to let go of a lion's tail in the African bush. A Pit Bull Terrier at sport in a nineteenth-century London pit once slew a hundred rats in five and a half minutes, a feat today's cute pet Jack Russell Terrier is probably capable of duplicating.

Today's terrier mutts have been chosen by their owners—rich and poor—for their ability to accomplish more sensible modern tasks such as watching TV, barking at the door, and providing fifteen to forty pounds of curly-haired unconditional love. All with a dash of that famous terrier gallantry.

Descriptions and Standards of the Terrier Mutt

The Airedale Mix

If terriers are bounce to the ounce, Airedale mixes are bound for the pound. A large, active, curly-coated, long-legged, high-maintenance dog. The King of the Terrier Mutts. Unlike the slick purebred pictures, the Airedale and its mixes can be dustballs. A tumbleweed of a dog, wiry hair exploding out everywhere. Combing, you gotta love it. This is an athletic, capable, clownish, protective home-and-hearth hybrid, but you must keep his barbershop appointments. Dead ringer for: a Standard Poodle–Labrador Retriever mix.

The American Staffordshire Terrier Mix

The breeders of the Amstaff worked hard to create a much more stable, calm, slower-to-fire pet after the Pit Bull Terrier horror headlines of the 1970s. The Amstaff is not to be confused with the less predictable Pit Bull Terrier. When considering a mix, make sure it really has Amstaff genes, mixed with something softer. A dead ringer for: Boxer and Bulldog mixes. (See Pit Bull Terrier mix.)

The Benji-Type

Benji the movie mutt is adorable, but remember that she is incredibly demanding, and she is a hero. This is the essential mien of the terrier mix. Terriers are fire. They ignite any mix, adding energy, opinion, feistiness, courage. Terrier mix persistence can range from the true war hero to the type who deluges the local paper with letters to the editor.

The Border Terrier Mix

The Border Terrier is a cute-as-a-mutton-chop Scottish farm dog who supplies oodles of terrier charm and pluck without a mean bone in his small body, unless you're a rat. If you can find a mix, adopt him. But this breed is rare. You're probably seeing things. What you're probably seeing is a Fox Terrier mix.

The Cairn Terrier Mix.

Toto in *The Wizard of Oz* was a Cairn. A Cairn mix will likely be stalwart, loyal, bold, and true. (Pulling the curtain on the Wizard was a characteristic Cairn plucky move.) Shorter legs in a mix may be a good sign—they can't get up on the counter quite as easily. A small, big-hearted dog who will bark at the mail carrier and protect you from burglars and flying monkeys.

The Bull Terrier–Jack Russell Terrier Mix

The Bull Russell Terrier. Like Bill Russell, the legendary Boston Celtics basketball player, this dog is a dominating presence. General Patton loved Bull Terriers, which is fitting: the Bull Russell is the General Patton of dogs. A Sherman Tank, look-out-here-I-come, ball-chasin', door-barkin', counter-bouncin', canine entertainment center juggernaut. A ton of dog. Train him early, train him late. He won't listen.

The Fox Terrier Mix

Can be a dead ringer for a Jack Russell Terrier cross. A dog with a mission, but more gentlemanly and polite than the Jack.

The Irish Terrier Mix

A handsome, medium-sized, and courageous terrier who excelled in ratting, guarding, and World War I action. No

Shadow

matter what similarities these activities bear to raising children, the purebred may be too much dog for a typical household. But an Irish mix could be a charming, if bold, dog.

The Jack Russell Terrier Mix

The Jack Russell is the terrier's terrier. A rat catcher to the second power. So quarrelsome are these terriers they can't run a race without stopping midway to brawl. Almost any mixed-breed mate would soften a pure Jack and leave you, hopefully, with distilled cuteness. Call a sweeter female Jack mix a Jane Russell Terrier.

The Lakeland Terrier Mix

From the bucolic Lake District of northern England comes this indomitable foxhunter who likes to pick fights with other dogs. A rare mix. Very useful to hardscrabble farmers of the last century, but perhaps not to you unless the mixing process softens her considerably.

The Miniature Schnauzer Mix

The Miniature Schnauzer mix tends to be one of the more laid-back terrier mixes. Steffi, a Mini we know, jumps four feet off the ground like a pogo stick when it's time for a walk. This is terrier for "laid-back." Schnauzers, a German breed, are the outlanders among the British Isles—dominated terriers, and are one of the few that

Heidi

The Pit Bull Terrier Mix

Like John Wayne in *The Quiet Man*, this mutt won't start a fight, but he finishes all of them. Despite their reputation, pits are not nasty dogs by any means. Musclebound, loyal love machines who should never be provoked around other animals. However, Pit Bulls can range from sweet and reliable dogs to police-blotter items waiting to happen, so be careful when adopting a mix. (See American Staffordshire Terrier mix.)

The Scottish Terrier Mix

The Irish bred their terriers to be sprightly and gay; the Scottish to be more dour and aloof. So it is with the strong-willed Scottish Terrier. The Scottie is small but don't dare tell him. His mother says he's single-minded. Warms up slowly to outsiders. Self-important. Never lets you forget his image is everywhere among collectors since FDR owned Fala. A Scotty mixed with a more eager people dog could be a very charming critter.

never "went to ground" for rodents. The Schnauzer mix is a playful, barky, fun-loving, one-owner creature. Schnauzer-avec-something generally makes a good dog.

The Norfolk Terrier Mix

Adorable. This breed looks like a Gund toy, and their personality matches their looks. The mix is a plush toy without the trademark tag. Blessedly, a slow draw for a terrier. Mixes are relatively rare. If you find one, adopt her and ask questions later. The Norfolk's kissing cousin, the Norwich Terrier, was the same breed until the 1970s and brings virtually the same flavor to a mix. Like onion instead of scallions.

The Terrier-Beagle Mix

Sometimes called the Teagle. In his youth, hide the rabbits. In his golden years, hide the hors d'oeuvres. At any age, this mutt has a big heart and a big mouth. A very barky dog who eats a lot. More Oral than your toothbrush.

The Terrier–Chow Chow Mix

Keep your hands inside the car at all times. A potentially devoted, formidable one-person dog. For that person, potentially the best dog of all. Did we say potentially? A combustible mix. Will have little use for or interest in people other than her owner.

The Three-Legged Terrier

There's no room in official breeding standards for three-legged dogs, but there's a place for them here, as well as in many mutt-loving homes. Politically incorrect name: dog stools. We know a stout and charming three-legged American Staffordshire Terrier mix. Although dogs can and do adapt to three-leggedness, the Amstaff mix hardly notices. This incredibly athletic, no-pain-threshold mutt doesn't take no for an answer. She is one of the few dogs who could probably adapt to one-leggedness.

The Welsh Terrier Mix

A handsome mini-Airedale in appearance but somewhat hard to handle. The breed was created to protect livestock and crops from foxes, weasels, hares, and rats. If you don't have livestock or crops, look for a more companionable mix.

The West Highland White Terrier Mix

Lost out to Cairn Terrier for the part of Toto in *The Wizard of Oz*. A Westie mix is an adorable little dynamo, soft as silk but no softie at heart. Likely to be a wizard ratter. Very similar to the Cairn Terrier, with which it was largely crossed in nineteenth-century Scotland. A mix with a Samoyed or other north-country dog could be a wonderful pet. A North-Wester. (If the Pekingese or Chinese Crested Dog is part of the mix, call him a Nor-Easter.)

Tuppence

🐕 Benji: Shelter Dog to Superstar

SCENE: Paris, a five-star restaurant. A film star is in the house tonight. A brown, furry, fifteen-pound dog of mixed blood and orphan background sits over a white tablecloth, swaddled in pink napkin, being spoon-fed small sliced pieces of filet mignon.

MCMXCVI Benji Assoc.

From Pound Dog to Proud Dog— Benji shakes paws with President Carter

As his attendants well know, Benji, off screen, is hardly the hunted. The mongrel mogul rides limos, jets to the Cannes Film Festival, gives out Emmy Awards, and shakes paws with presidents.

How, in dog's name, did this happen? How did a doomed pound dog become the most gifted mixed-breed actor, most beloved mutt—very possibly the best-known dog of any type—in the history of the world?

In the lore of random-bred dogs, this is the classic wags-to-riches tale.

Benji's films have grossed more than $200 million. In the 1990s, Benji's movies are pulling in millions more in home video sales. Critics compare Benji's best acting, in *Benji the Hunted,* to that of Charlie Chaplin, Buster Keaton, and other silent screen legends, wordless wonders all. "We see more emotional range from this dog than you get from all the Brat Pack boys put together," *USA Today* once opined. Benji was the second animal (and the first mutt) inducted into the Animal Actors Hall of Fame, trailing only Lassie.

Benji's stardom has precedent in other Hollywood film legends.

If you're thinking Lana Turner, you're not the first to see notable parallels between the careers of Benji and the glamorous actress of the 1940s and 1950s. Both embodied the American dream: "Discovered" in dead-end California lives, each went on to remarkably enduring film careers spanning parts of three decades. Both were nominated once for the Academy Award (Lana for *Peyton Place;* Benji for, well, one of the songs in his movies.) Both dabbled in TV. Each became a "type" desired by millions of Americans.

Alas, only one was judged by *Time* magazine to be "the most lovable creature ever created by Hollywood," and also said by critics to possess the acting talent of "another Sir Laurence Olivier." (Hint: the other possessed the acting talent to earn the nickname "The Sweater Girl.")

Higgins, the mutt who would be Benji, was discovered in Burbank, California, in the early 1960s, just as Julia Jean Mildred Frances Turner was discovered at sixteen in a Hollywood malt shop in 1936. Frank Inn, Hollywood animal trainer of Arnold the Pig, told Higgins: You oughta be in pictures.

"I didn't really need him at the time," Inn said. "But I took him so he wouldn't have to be put to sleep."

Higgins debuted on *Petticoat Junction,* playing checkers with Uncle Joe and learning a new trick for the show every week for seven years. After a long and prosperous career as an animal actor, Higgins retired from *Petticoat Junction.*

In 1974, at the age of thirteen, in his nineties in human years, Higgins came out of retirement to star in *Benji.* Alas, Benji, by then known as "The Old Man," was never able to enjoy the phenomenon he had created. No sooner was the star reborn than he died, shortly after the release of the first movie.

Fortunately there was a litter of little Benjis waiting to succeed their dad. In the late 1970s, Frank Inn tried one after another of Benji's sons to follow in the pawprints of Benji—but none of the boys had the right acting stuff.

So it was that for the next twelve years, for the five subsequent Benji boffo hits, including *For the Love of Benji, Oh, Heavenly Dog!,* and *Benji the Hunted,* Christmas specials and a dozen TV shows, Benji, male lead, was played by his daughter!

By the time Benji II retired and Benji III took her place, there were so many Benji-related spawn that Benji III was "a great-great-great-grand nephew" of "The Old Man." Or something like that. "I don't know how many greats or how many grands there are," confesses North Carolina filmmaker Joe Camp, who created Benji. Just as it's impossible to tell what kind of dog Benji really is, "there's no way to be sure," Camp says.

Freda

In 1989, her mother died in a fall down the cellar steps. In 1991, her father, eighty-four years old, committed suicide. In 1992, she was beaten up badly on a lovely morning in the city. A month later, her brother died of AIDS.

"I always loved the Book of Job," says poet Maralyn Lois Polak. "Eventually, I lived through it."

Unhappily for Job, he never had Freda to bail him out. But that's getting ahead of the story. First, Maralyn's husband left her—left her with a $10 Cocker Spaniel–Beagle mix he had named Arpeggio (the cat was Allegro). After the split, Maralyn renamed the dog Froggy. Froggy lived a long, happy life, proudly wearing his eight vests, twelve T-shirts, and London Fog raincoat in Philadelphia's Rittenhouse Square.

When Froggy died, Maralyn passed sadly over all the dogs in the animal shelter, until the last cage. "A perky, spunky puppy challenged me: Hey, Look at me! I'm female;

Freda

Elena Bouvier

you wanted a male. I'm white; you wanted a black one. I'm a terrier; you wanted a Beagle. I'm yours! We had an instant connection."

The stray had been found wandering city streets, abused, totally wild, eating trash. She cowered from human contact, didn't know how to walk on a leash or eat from a bowl. Her name was Freda, "an old Jewish grandmother name" Maralyn wanted to change. But when Maralyn walked the dog home, a street artist looked up from his easel at the new dog and said, "What's her name? Freda?" It was fate.

Nowadays Freda listens to opera, eats vegetables and herbs, poses for artists, dances on her hind legs, visits a human chiropractor for back problems (he once prescribed six weeks cage rest in a playpen; Maralyn slept on the floor next to Freda). Freda's essential character combines the combativeness of her partial Jack Russell Terrier bloodlines with a wild flirtatiousness for men, making her, perhaps, the first Jane Russell Terrier.

"In my career as a permanently single person," Maralyn says, "Freda is my gauge to who is good and who is not. She sits on their lap and kisses the men she likes."

One date told Maralyn to get rid of the dog. She got rid of the man.

🐕 Empress Molly

"Here is the story of a child of the streets who captured our hearts and has risen to be queen of all she surveys.

"This is our Molly Mag.

"There was this picture on the front page of the local paper, the *Carteret* (North Carolina) *New Times*. Large eyes looked out of a dark mass. The caption said only, 'Please.' The dark mass was eight newborn puppies gathered around their dam at the animal shelter.

"The lady said, 'There's my dog,' and early the next morning we were at the gates of the shelter. When she announced she had come for her dog, the lady was told the young ones had to be weaned before the mother could leave.

"Her response: 'I shall return. Meanwhile start calling her Molly.'

"The poor little animal weighed under thirteen pounds and looked like she had been dragged through a knothole and wrung out. On the appointed day we were at the gates early with checkbook at the ready, but behold, on the opening day of 'Seniors Adopt a Pet Program,' we were the first and everything was on the house. This included being featured on the local TV.

"We took her to the vet for the final checkout. His advice, 'Take her back. She's loaded with heartworm.' He wasn't optimistic and that was eight years ago.

"When Molly came to us a ball was a threat. She had no concept of play. Terrified of cars. After all, she'd been dumped. Now she's been to Pennsylvania and Florida with no problem. The phrase 'Go in the car' gets action. She owns all the land and guards it jealously. She runs raccoons out of her azaleas at night. She hates all big dogs with a passion. It took her a while to accept me but she's still leery of men.

"In her declining years she is our baby and we are her charges. Molly thinks she's died and gone to heaven. We are happy to have made it so."

Gene Dugan

Empress Molly

🐕 Anne and Zoe

Once not long ago, in one of the lost neighborhoods of Brooklyn, two little girls playing in a parking lot wept when they discovered the victim of a satanic ritual, begging for life.

The discarded creature was, when they wiped away the blood and the filth, a puppy. A tiny golden puppy, no bigger than their hands, its right front leg chopped in half. The girls never hesitated: they bundled up the puppy and took her to the ASPCA.

Veterinarians "went nuts, they put fluids into her, they got her back," says ASPCA President Roger Caras. "You don't want a dog with a stump. They try to walk on it and are constantly bumping into things and it's no good. So they took the leg off cleanly at the shoulder like they always do." The good people at the ASPCA rehabilitated her and put her up for adoption as a three-legged dog, a "Shepherd mix."

Four or five months passed. No one wanted the three-legged dog. "You'd think people's hearts would go out to a three-legged dog, but it's not the case."

The three-legged puppy's death, in the way animal shelters handle pet overpopulation, was scheduled many times. Caras forbade it. "I said under no circumstances will that dog be put down. I'll take her if nobody else will."

Roger Caras has already taken four Greyhounds nobody else would, along with seven other dogs, cats, birds, horses, cows, llamas. Caras blames the rescue of thirty-odd pets on his wife, Jill. Jill put out an SOS to their friend and neighbor, Anne Graul. Anne and her husband, Tom, already had five dogs.

Make that six.

Nowadays, the three-legged puppy lives in the horse country of northern Maryland on an eighty-six-acre estate with twelve horses, six peacocks, and fifteen cats. The Grauls named her Zoe, so she could play with Chloe, a three-legged mongrel rescued by Caras's daughter, Pamela Rupert.

"As far as we know, dogs can't count and they don't know they should have four legs," Caras says. "Zoe and Chloe get by splendidly on three. The three-legged dogs are the sweetest dogs you've ever seen."

When Zoe tires of hobbling about, she is chauffered in the 1962 Bentley. The Grauls took a picture of Zoe grinning as happy dogs do, her lone front leg hanging out of the Bentley, under the banner, "Living Well Is the Best Revenge."

🐕 The Incredible Journey

Forget the movie version. This is a true incredible journey: two stray dogs, a feral cat, and a homeless woman on the streets for two years together, looking for a home.

Patricia K. Myers has pictures of the shack she lived in on the South Platte River in Colorado when she wasn't wandering the streets of Denver; snapshots of the shopping cart where she stored her belongings and tethered her dogs. Now the Polaroids show the dogs and cats curled up together on a nice wooden floor, in a home with a roof and walls.

"Baby Bear, Pancho, Tasha, and I all got together in 1991, and are all still together," Myers says proudly.

Patricia was a nurse's aide in Colorado, but she developed back problems in 1988, lost her job, and ended up homeless. She was alone on the streets for three years. Then, one day, she saw a pack of homeless dogs foraging the same ground homeless folks do in Denver.

"I made friends with the dogs, feeding them sandwiches from a local homeless shelter," Patricia recalls. "In time a large beautiful black dog with white markings became mine, and so did her companion dog, a scruffy terrier mix. Baby Bear and Pancho were inseparable." A few days later, a couple of homeless friends brought Patricia a scabrous kitten they'd found. "In a matter of days I acquired two wonderful dogs and my beautiful cat Tasha (who was anything but beautiful then!)," Patricia says.

Her pets were Patricia's salvation, and saviors, time and again. One night, "I awoke to a growl and saw a man leaning over me with a butcher knife." Pancho, growling, was chained to a grocery cart, but Baby Bear chased the robber away. Another time, a night attacker punched the sleeping Patricia in the face, bloodied her nose, broke her glasses, kicked Baby Bear savagely, downing the ninety-pound dog. "This time it was Pancho to the rescue!" Patricia says. "Pancho bit the man on the ankle,

Baby Bear, Pancho, and Tasha   *Patricia K. Myers*

was kicked in the face (losing several teeth), then came back and ripped the man's arm from elbow to wrist." The attacker fled.

When the homeless camps on the South Platte River were bulldozed, Patricia was offered a place in a homeless shelter, no pets allowed. "In a shelter, you get only warmth," she said. "My dogs and cats give me warmth and love me." She chose to stay on the streets with her animal family.

Eventually, Patricia was able to rent a duplex that allows pets. She's living on disability from an injured back and arm. It's not much, but it's enough to keep her family of four together. "I can't imagine any of us being separated," Patricia says. "I consider my mutts to be heroes, and the best companions a woman could have."

McFly and Leaky Peter

Sometimes Mother Nature brings two or more sweet breeds together in a marvelous mutt. Sometimes she doesn't. Sometimes, somehow, a Bull Terrier–Jack Russell Terrier gets born. Somehow, the resulting little Bull Russell finds love.

His name is McFly, or Mister Mack. Wanna make something of it?

"He looks like a rough-coated Jack Russell on steroids," says owner Liz Sharpe of Glenn Dale, Maryland. "I refer to him as a Bull Russell when people ask. He is twenty-nine and a half pounds of jaunty gristle and testosterone, and true to both his breeds, cannot be either bribed or daunted. Another expression for this is: 'Flunked obedience school.' Fortunately, he is extremely amiable." Unless you're one of the neighborhood squirrels.

As Mister Mack is hard and tough, so his younger brother, Leaky Peter Pepperpot, is soft and, well, all wet. Leaky Peter is an Australian Cattle Dog–American Eskimo (Spitz) cross. "With his tail down, he looks like a slightly ratty Cattle Dog," Sharpe says. "When that prehensile plume curls up and over the other way, he's definitely some kind of mutant off-color Spitzoid."

Leaky Peter, unfortunately, earned his name—"from a reflexive watering of my feet anytime I accidentally assumed too dominant a posture during his early years," Sharpe says.

"Pete, like his mother, is over-anxious to please."

McFly

🐕 Heidi "The Wonder Puppy"

Although mixed-breed dogs are often healthier than purebreds, a dog's life isn't always fair. Tina Marie and Dante Flamminio found out the hard way.

"My husband and I kept hearing the neurologist's own words over and over," says Tina Marie. "Well, Mr. and Mrs. Flamminio, if your dog was a human, she'd be a special-needs child. We were the parents of Forrest Gump with four legs."

The Flamminios had adopted Heidi, a terrier mix with a wise old-soul face, from the SPCA. They had never had a dog. "Her coal black eyes, deerlike ears, and coiled pig tail won us over," Tina Marie says. "But we never dreamed that a dog would teach Dante and me anything about love, devotion, and faith."

On Christmas Day 1994, far from home, Heidi went into a seizure. A vet said it was canine distemper, often fatal. "I held Heidi's frail and limp body in my arms for the entire five-and-a-half-hour ride home," Tina Marie

Heidi

Tina (Angelo) Flamminio

says. "Her sad, dark eyes stared at me. I kept telling her how much mommy and daddy loved her."

Back home, Dante and Tina Marie took their last pictures together with Heidi, "held her and cried like two babies," Tina Marie says.

With heavy heart, they took Heidi to their local vet to be put down. The vet confirmed distemper, then handed Tina Marie a huge book, pointing to one sentence: "Many owners put their dogs to sleep much too early when diagnosed with distemper."

"That's all I needed to hear," Tina Marie said. "We took Heidi home." First they took Heidi to their church. Unable to find a priest to bless her, they held the little dog together on the steps outside and prayed that God wouldn't let her die.

"The first week Dante and I were up most of the night, feeding Heidi, listening to her breathing, carrying Heidi outside because she was too weak to walk up or down stairs," Tina Marie says. "I kept telling Heidi that she was my 'Wonder Puppy.'"

Heidi lost peripheral vision, strength in her legs, and a bit of memory forever, but the virus eventually ran its course.

"She walks into walls and furniture, drops on all fours like a camel at times, and can't quite remember what she is supposed to do outside," Tina Marie said. "And the tail that once coiled like a pig's now hangs straight down between her legs.

"But the disease didn't take away her ability to love unconditionally, make us laugh, and bring joy to our lives. To me, Heidi will always be our Wonder Puppy."

Madeleine Mary, Mother of Dog

She ain't no hero, Rita Mary allows. She isn't so pretty, Rita Mary acknowledges. "But at seventeen, this great American mutt rules a house in which she is the oldest, and by far the smallest of four dogs."

Madeleine Mary, terrier mix, bosses around the giants—two Irish Wolfhounds and a Chesapeake Bay Retriever. She's outlived a houseful of other dogs. Twenty-five people

Madeleine Mary

Rita Mary Hanly

came to her Sweet Sixteen party. Maddie wore pearls and got lots of gifts. Maddie is deaf now. But still when her human, Dr. Rita Mary Hanly, is upset or crying, Maddie "will come and rest her paws on my knee, and gaze at me with soft brown Madeleine eyes, letting me know that she understands."

By far the smartest of the ten dogs Rita Mary has had, Maddie uses a special "pay attention!" bark in crises. Maddie has deemed only three occasions worthy of this special bark in seventeen years. Once when her collar got caught on a low branch in the yard. Another time when a neighbor's house was being burglarized. And the third time when an older red dog, Buffy, one of the many dogs Maddie eventually outlived, had had surgery. When Buffy came home, he slipped into semiconsciousness and Rita Mary, a physician, injected him with the proper drug to make him better. It was late at night. Rita Mary put Buffy on some blankets in the master bathroom, set an alarm for two hours, and went to sleep.

An hour later, Maddie jumped on the bed and awakened her human with her "pay attention!" bark. "I jumped up," Rita Mary remembers. "Buffy was walking around, perky, as if he had never had a problem. Maddie told me Buffy was okay!"

Big, deer-like eyes—better to beg with, my dear.

Blond highlighted hair because it brings out the luster of a strand of pearls.

Short nose because it's a sign of good breeding.

Delicate bones for striking poses.

Samantha Fahnstock

Bailey

THE TOY MUTTS

Being possessed by a toy mutt is like adorning oneself with an impressive yet playful 1-carat rock; it has a distant relationship to the breathtaking, becursed Hope Diamond, yet is much less trouble to own.

The famous purebred toys—haughty, sprightly, stubborn, sensitive, legendary, and very expensive—have endured far too many centuries of royal pampering, court treachery, and quarterly downsizing to ever be completely normal pets.

The Bichon Frise, for instance, was perfumed by Henry III, painted by Goya, beloved by Napoleon III—and fell to street life as an organ grinder's surrogate monkey. A Pomeranian named Turi was summoned to lie beside Queen Elizabeth when she drew her last breath. Long before her fateful demise, Marie Antoinette lost her head over a Papillon (French for Butterfly). Mary Queen of Scots' beloved English Toy Spaniel actually had to watch from the scaffold while Mary was executed. A Pug, named Fortune, was enlisted by the imprisoned Josephine to carry secret messages under his collar to her husband, Napoleon. Imagine the stress!

Today's toy mutts come with a scent of this dangerous legacy, a sniff of the purebred's Dom Pérignon, but are more sensible, their fanciers claim. Economical, too.

Toy mutts fit comfortably in all laps, regardless of size. (The famous "one size sits all" guarantee.) Their great secret is they can pass for Royal Pekingese, Yorkies, ungroomed Toy Poodles, Maltese, and Shih Tzus, since few laypeople can tell these breeds apart.

Descriptions and Standards of the Toy Mutt

The Cavalier King Charles Spaniel Mix

A rare mix, but if you were to find one, he'd add sweetness and light to your life. The breed's tail never stops moving. One of the most charming breeds with kids, the King Charles is headed for overpopularity and genetic ruination. Happily, adopting a random-bred version from the animal shelter will largely protect you from that.

The Chihuahua Mix

If not part of their family, keep your gloves on at all times. They can be nippy. Look for a softening of the Chihuahua through random mating with, say, anything else. All mutts are eternally grateful for being rescued from the pound, but the Chihuahua thinks you're the one who ought to be grateful. Why such attitude? While other toys were lapdogs for kings, early Chihuahua mixes were so loved by the Aztecs they were sacrificed to guide the souls of the dead. Yikes. With friends like that, who needs dog pounds?

The Cocker Spaniel–Miniature Poodle Mix

The Cock-a-Poo. An incredibly charming combination. Classic mutts have been deliberately made for so long they border on breed status. At their best, an advertise-ment for hybrid vigor, combining the good qualities of both breeds: the sweetness of the Cocker; the intelligence and charm of the Poodle. At their worst, they're neurotic, yappy, aggressive little things. Be careful. A less contrived mutt may be advisable.

The Lhasa Apso–Pekingese Mix

The Lhasa-Peke. The Lhasa talks only to the Peke and the Peke talks only to God. The Pekes of civilized old China aren't interested in status because they're the best. A Peke we knew, Mr. Ying, abhorred training class, and sat behind his chair facing

Emily

the wall until summoned. "Oh, God, *okay*," he'd mutter, then do everything perfectly. The haughty, aloof Peke combined with the stubborn, standoffish, more aggressive Lhasa is likely to think very well of himself and quite a bit less of you.

The Lhasa Apso–Poodle–Cocker Spaniel Mix

One more revolution in the spin cycle past the Cock-a-Poo. The added Lhasa genes may be just enough to work vigorous hybrid magic. If you get Poodle intelligence, Cocker charm, plus the loyalty and devotion of a Lhasa, you have one heck of a mixed-breed dog. The Lotsa-Cock-a-Poo.

The Lhasa Apso–Toy Poodle Mix

Does the Poodle get around, or what? Among the Napoleonic toys, this is a fortunate mix: the Poodle will soften the Lhasa's Olympic opinion of herself and make a mix that's more willing to please. The Lhasa will contribute some calmness and decorum for those difficult first two years. Training a Toy Poodle puppy can be like trying to catch a firefly in a jar.

The Maltese–Toy Poodle Mix

The Malted Poo. Engaging, demanding, ambitious, and opinionated. Get the dog trick book out. This is a dog to teach. A hoop-jumping, fire-walking, hind-leg-

Ziggy

Courteasy Kenneth White, Arizona Humane Society & the H.S.U.S.

dancing, vaudeville-starring little dog. This is all very unamusing to the Lhasa-Peke.

The Miniature Schnauzer–Toy Poodle Mix

The Schnoodle. A noisy, charming, bouncy, sensitive, creative, precocious little pooch. High SAT score, especially the verbal side.

The Papillon Mix

The French Butterfly dog, devoted, smart, willing, a terrific little dog. Will probably learn a hundred tricks from you and will teach you two hundred of her own. Very, very bright mutt. Yet more proof that good things come in small packages.

The Pekingese-Poodle Mix

The Peke-a-Poo. The Empress of China marries the court jester. A very bright mix capable of many tricks but won't do them. Don't call her a Peke-a-Poo to her face. The Queen of Mutts says, "Don't talk babytalk to me."

The Pomeranian Mix

Cranky for a toy mix, noisy and independent. If you like your petit four with a dash of red pepper, this is the dessert mix for you.

The Poodle–Basset Hound Mix

A form of Cupid's arrow that hits you very slowly. Sweet, sweet dog. All the Poodle's intelligence mixed with the Basset's s-l-o-w, l-a-i-d–b-a-c-k charm. A perfect mix to be a therapy dog, which is in fact what the Psychotherapoodle in this chapter is.

The Poodle–Welsh Terrier Mix

You keep thumbing through your illustrated guide to every AKC breed. You can't escape the conclusion. Muttley *has* to be a Welsh-Poodle. You're dreamin'. Chances are it's a Schnauzer-Poodle, a charming, if more common, mutt type.

The Pug-Dachshund Mix

Adorable, friendly, sweet, comical, entertaining. There's nothing funnier than the obsessively friendly, people-loving Pug. A Pug contains good canine ingredients. You add it to anything and it comes out fine. One Pug flaw: their short nose causes them to swallow too much air while eating, causing flatulence. A mongrelized version with Dachshund influences will likely have a longer muzzle and be less gassy. Oddly enough, a dead ringer for: a Beagle mix.

The Shih Tzu Mix

Unlike the imperious Lhasa Apso, this adorable little dog was not bred as a guard dog. Even better, Shih Tzu mixes consider the world to be their oyster, and you the pearl.

The Yorkshire Terrier Mix

This little English dog struts around your house like he pays the mortgage, which in fact he thinks he does. Yorkies have famously high opinions of themselves, which their owners find quite amusing. It's charming to get a whiff of this massive ego-mini dog in a mongrel who has other traits too, like humility. Any mix would make a Yorkie more humble.

Mutts in the Crusades

Dogs, no doubt, will accompany astronauts to Mars as they once accompanied knights on the Great Crusades. The tomb of Sir Roger de Trumpington in Cambridgeshire, England, includes a full-length portrait of that thirteenth-century Crusader engraved in brass. At his feet, clothed in chain mail booties, "crouches a small dog of indeterminate type," according to dog researchers Denenberg and Seidman, "flicking its rather enlongated tail and gazing up at the knight reverentially."

🐕 The Psychotherapoodle

Up the stairs of the New York City prewar building they come, men and women haunted by violence suffered in Castro's Cuba, in Vietnam, in the Holocaust, seeking comfort and healing.

Their appointments are with the psychotherapist Robbye Stuart-Russell, fifty-two. But at the top of the stairs they are greeted by the analyst's longtime psychotherapy aid, Inanna. Inanna, nine years old, is a curly, black, thirty-seven-pound Poodle mix. The Psychotherapoodle.

Sigmund Freud had a Chow Chow, Jofi, in his office. The purebred Jofi sniffed disdainfully at some patients and turned away, according to Freud's son, Martin, signaling "a strong impression there was something wrong with that caller's character."

Inanna does it differently.

"I open the door and she just takes off and runs out, gives them the puppy crazies, everything wiggles," Robbye says. "She jumps up and down and cries, 'Oh boy, you're here! You're here! It's wonderful you're here!'

"My co-therapist can do things that would be inappropriate or professionally unethical for me to do."

Lying on a pillow in a corner of Robbye's Upper West Side office, Inanna gets up to comfort anyone who cries or seems anxious. Once, the Poodle mix was called in on the case of a nine-year-old girl who couldn't talk to her therapist about being molested.

"The little girl was lying on the floor, crying, when we entered the room," Robbye remembers. "Inanna just walked over and lay down next to her. The child calmed herself, petted Inanna, and was able to talk to Inanna in time. The girl had been molested in a park, and had a fear of going outside. Eventually, we got her outside in a park, throwing tennis balls to Inanna."

Robbye rescued Inanna eight and a

Robbye Stuart-Russell

Inanna

half years ago from an ASPCA adoption van when the therapist herself was depressed.

"I got her at a point in my life when I'd experienced a very painful end to a relationship, the death of a close friend, a death in the family," Robbye says. "She's my best friend in a way only animals can be. She asks for nothing. She gives everything. She just wants to please. As a friend of mine said, she's a fairy goddess."

 Buffy and Bubbles

Every morning at a mobile home park in Riverside, California, Buffy and Bubbles take their constitutional, a long walk with Dorothy around the local Kmart.

Buffy is a white Poodle-Maltese who is almost eighty years old by human standards. Bubbles is a black Pekingese-Lhasa Apso who is also getting on in years. Dorothy is Dorothy Gouyd, seventy-six, a wonderful human by human standards, although she doesn't walk her girls as far as she used to.

Bubbles and Buffy

Dorothy Gouyd

"Buffy and Bubbles want to get home these days for a nap," Dorothy says, "and I get tired now because I have to carry Mia, a very old Pekingese. Mia's owner died of cancer and I promised I'd care for her."

Buffy, Bubbles, and Dorothy are all now retired. But in Riverside, they haven't forgotten the little dogs who kept the old and sick entertained, or their owner, who kept her promises.

Dorothy was alone after her divorce, raised two children by herself, kept the books at St. Thomas Catholic Church for thirty-two years, volunteered for the Heart Association, Girl Scouts, *and* Boy Scouts for forty-five years. Then one day Dorothy visited the dog pound with her granddaughters and lost her heart to Buffy and Bubbles.

When the dogs were young, Dorothy took them to visit an old folks' home, and discovered a new purpose: spreading love as warm and constant as the Southern California sunshine.

Her girls had magic. "They love people, love children, love to be kissed," Dorothy says. "And people just love them back to pieces."

Why, you'd take Buffy into a room and she'd make a beeline for the most depressed person like a clown closing in on a sad child. Bubbles, who apparently broke the mold of both his dignified, aloof breeds, the Peke and the Lhasa, would leap up next to a veteran without legs and arms, putting a rare wide smile on the man's face. Mental patients who had never talked burst joyfully from their silence upon seeing Buffy and Bubbles.

The salt-and-pepper pups visited thirty-seven schools and hospitals a month for years. They made local TV appearances and, in 1991, Buffy and Bubbles appeared on Bob Hope's *Salute to American Pets*. In 1993, when Dorothy quit her job as director of the Riverside Humane Society pet therapy program, Buffy and Bubbles retired too.

Even now, Buffy and Bubbles "get very excited when someone visits" their mobile home, Dorothy says. "They do all their tricks."

⠀🐕 The Never-Ending Dog

Sometimes dogs never have the opportunity to save your life. Sometimes they just change it in small, important ways by simply being there.

Once in South Florida there was a little girl named Jill Francisco. When she was born there was a dog, George, at her side. George was a small shaggy dog who had always slept in mom's bed. But when Jill was born it seemed like George knew he had a different purpose now.

The Franciscos

George

Each day George would lie by the baby's crib. Every time Jill cried, George howled. When mom's boss came to see the baby, George almost bit her when she tried to pick Jill up. That was okay; George knew that mom didn't like her boss.

"George" was one of Jill's first words. When Jill became a little girl, five years old, George was her best friend. As time went on, Jill went to school and became so busy she paid less attention to George. "We seemed to grow apart," Jill remembers. "But I still loved him. I just didn't show it as much."

When she got older, Jill was so involved with her friends she didn't see much of George at all. George was slowing down now, but he always ran to see Jill whenever she

came home, wagging his tail so happily. "I still fed him ice cream when my mom wasn't looking," Jill said.

When George was fifteen years old, and Jill was twelve, George really started to age. All he did was sleep and bark to go out. Jill was annoyed by George, and didn't want to be around him. "Then he got cataracts in both eyes and his legs began to get weak," Jill said. "I wasn't really that worried about him but my mom seemed to be sometimes."

At sixteen, the family began calling him "the never-ending dog." As George aged, he was hard for Jill and her mom to take care of. He slept more and more, but he still wagged his tail whenever he saw Jill.

One morning when Jill was fourteen and George was almost seventeen, Jill heard her mom, Denise, say, "I think it's time. All he does is lie on the floor shaking." Jill thought she had outgrown George, but she was wrong. That day she ran to her mom and hugged her and said she would help take George to the vet's.

Once there was a dog named George. When George lay down for the last time, he had his girl at his side. When George moaned and cried, his girl cried too.

"That was the hardest trip I've ever made," Jill says. "I went in the room with George and my mom . . . and said goodbye to a friend I thought would never leave me."

Jill has three dogs, two cats, a bird, and a rabbit now, but the love she has for all of them doesn't match, she says, the love she has for George, the never-ending dog.

🐕 Ginger

On a typical afternoon at the Chase Memorial Nursing Home in Upstate New York, Ginger, the little house mutt, waddles out of her room and down the hallway, trying to decide which of the eighty patients to visit next, waiting patiently at the elevator if someone she wants to see lives on the second floor.

There are nursing homes in America that are sterile and cold, where the elderly are medicated, wither, and die. There are livelier homes touched by the joy of regular animal visits. Then there is the nursing home where Ginger, the tiny yellow lap mutt with big brown eyes, lives permanently, along with four house cats, a retired Greyhound racing dog, rabbits, and chinchillas. The shouts of children from the day-care center echo through the home, along with the song of more than one hundred parakeets, finches, cockatiels, and lovebirds kept by residents.

"Most nursing homes are set up to treat medical problems," says Dr. William Thomas, chief physician at Chase and creator of the Eden Alternative, copied by seventy-five nursing homes so far. "We're trying to answer several well-documented human needs. People have had companionship with animals for thousands of years; it's an ancient, powerful thing. Not visits from animals—full-time companionship. People need not just to be cared for, but to *care* for other living things. And they need spontaneity in their lives. Ginger, by bringing all of these things, is literally saving lives."

The first year after Ginger arrived, Chase Memorial reported a 15 percent drop in its death rate. Infection rates dropped about 50 percent. Staff turnover rates fell 26 percent. The use of medications dropped 50 percent. By the second year, the death rate had dropped 25 percent.

"Ginger is the most adorable dog you'll ever see," says Judy Meyers-Thomas, Dr. Thomas's wife, who introduced many of the animals into the Eden Alternative. "She's soooo loving, lovable, and outgoing. She rides around on the Birdmobile, an old medical cart converted to feed the birds, visiting patients. She sleeps in beds, puts her paws up on wheelchairs, hops in laps. She's this tiny cuddly fluffy thing with sad brown eyes and you just can't *not* pet her. Mutts have really been the best kind of dogs for this. You don't need purebreds."

Ginger

A frail woman in her eighties, who left the home for a surgery from which patients often never return, demanded daily updates on the condition of Petey and Tweety, her parakeets, and "my dog, Ginger." She had to make it back to take care of Ginger, she said. She did.

A tiny Italian woman, also in her eighties, robbed of speech by a stroke, terrified of dogs, learned to love petting Ginger on her lap every day. "Ginger is a marvel with people who can't speak," Dr. Thomas says. "These people are really cut off from human companionship without language; but they don't need language to have companionship with Ginger."

None of the nurses had ever heard W.P., a bald, bespectacled man in his seventies, utter a single word. W.P. had an advanced case of Parkinson's disease, which severely restricts movement. Then one day Ginger leapt onto W.P.'s lap, triggering the kind of emotion that can reattach, even for a moment, the connections broken by the disease. The old man cried, clear as a summer's day, "What a cute little doggie!"

Ginger, the medical staff marvels, seems to know who needs her most, as she makes her way up and down the elevator, room to room.

Recalled Ardath Hendrickson, eighty-eight: "One or two times when I didn't feel good that little dog would come in and look at me as if to say, 'I'm sorry you're feeling bad.'"

Luther the Lilliputian Mastiff

Half the joy of owning a mutt is answering the question "What kind of dog is that?" We know of a mongrel named Justa. What kind of dog is that? "Just a dog," says her happy owner. Another mutt goes by the moniker Can't Hardly. What kind of dog is *that?* Grinning, his owner responds, "You can't hardly tell." Other mongrel owners will tell you with a straight face, if you are preoccupied with knowing their dog's breed, that they own a Black Forest Terrier.

Patricia Long owns a Lilliputian Mastiff. Actually, he's a Schnauzer-Poodle mix, which ought to be a bouncy, pleasing little creature to judge by his ancestry. But one of the charms of mixes is they don't always match expectations. If a Lilliputian Mastiff sounds like something mythical that Gulliver brought back, a very tiny specimen who thinks mightily of himself, well, that's Luther.

Luther "meets all the breed requirements of the Lilliputian Mastiff," says Patricia, tongue firmly planted in cheek. "He is at the top limit for the breed, weighing in at twenty pounds, but his fearlessness and ferocious barking make him a prime example of the breed. He enjoys terrorizing all other dogs until they acknowledge that he is, indeed, Emperor of the Entire Universe. Like many dogs with a unique heritage, his high intelligence allows him to outthink and outmaneuver our purebreds, two Bernese Mountain Dogs. He excels in training his two people, and bends us to his will at every turn."

Patricia found Luther in a park on Martin Luther King Day (hence the name Luther) five years ago. "He had been practicing his sad Benji face," Long says, "which made it

Patricia Long

Luther

absolutely impossible for me to leave the half-starved puppy with ice-covered dreadlocks." Luther has scared off one burglar, alerted the Longs to a robber who got into the house in the evening while they were at home, and even stopped a stranger from breaking into a neighbor's car. "So our little Pit-Poodle has more than paid for his own upkeep," Long says.

Lucky

Marguerite Mary Hill found Lucky in the SPCA trailer that stops on the corner every Saturday morning. "They bring the animals back twice and if no one adopts them, then they are put to sleep. That's all I needed to hear. I paid the man and took Lucky home and named him Lucky because I knew I was lucky to get him.

"I knew I could not have a dog because I lived in a duplex, so I tried to hide him from my landlord. But a neighbor told him I had Lucky and he told me either I have him put to sleep or out I go. I looked down at Lucky.

"Lucky was a very mistreated dog. When I took him to

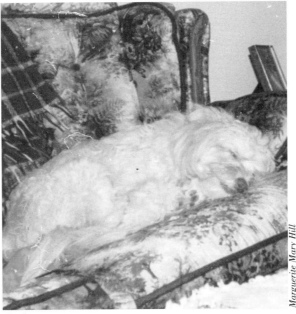

Lucky

Marguerite Mary Hill

the vet to have him neutered, he said Lucky had cigarette burns on his face and knife wounds on his back. When people ask me what kind of dog he is I say he is a mutt, but he is my mutt.

"There's not a human being in the world who could give me as much as Lucky, as he is my best friend and protector. There is not enough money in the world that anyone could give me for him. There is nothing created by God that better teaches us the meaning of love and loyalty than a dog.

"Lucky and I thank you for hearing our story. Ninety percent of this dog is spirit.

"I told the landlord I would rather have *him* put to sleep. I found another apartment and took Lucky with me."

Big brain to
figure out
how to open
doors.

Serious eyes;
"Can't you
see I'm
working?"

Tail up—Happi-
ness=Work=
Happiness.

Linda Caamaño

Chelsea

Alert ears
because
nothing gets
past them.

Strong legs
from
constant
movement.

THE HERDING MUTTS

Herding mutts, once humble Old World sheep and cattle dogs, have become rich, famous, and beguiling New Age stars. America, what a country!

Herding hybrids make grand entertainers and great athletes. Many of our mongrel media stars follow in the pawprints of herders Lassie and Rin Tin Tin. Herding dogs are a perfect temperamental match for the twentieth century, the classic mutt of our time: smart, intense, workaholic, mobile, adaptive, restless, light on their feet.

Seemingly antiquated sheepdog skills have allowed these sleepless mutts to adapt wonderfully to sheepless society. Herders thrill us with their speed and agility (Australian Shepherd mixes dominate the Frisbee dog championships); with their intelligence (Border Collies are the smartest dogs and Border Collie mixes the smartest mutts, according to *The Intelligence of Dogs.*); and with their zealous drive to protect and retrieve, especially family members. (See *Lassie* reruns, re: finding and bringing back Timmy.) With such lineage, no wonder a Collie mutt, Murray, steals our hearts on NBC's *Mad About You.* If ever a dog could find its way through the Internet, it'd be an Aussie–Border Collie cross.

The herders include the most noble yet commonest dog of all, the classic pound pooch, noted in shelters as the Shepherd X, the German Shepherd mix.

Descriptions and Standards of the Herding Mutt

The Australian Cattle Dog Mix

This hydrogen bomb bundle of energy has the ability, agility, and crazed intensity—smoothed out just a bit in a mysterious mongrel blend—to dominate the sport of Frisbee dogs in the 1990s or herd sheep with style, as the picture shows. Simply put, the Michael Jordan of dogs.

The Australian Cattle Dog–American Eskimo (Spitz) Dog Mix

A very unusual cross, highly unlikely these two would ever meet, but one has been reported to us. An active, barky, shy, slightly wacko dog is a distinct possibility.

The Belgian Shepherd Mix

Belgian Shepherds, divided into four varieties in their native Belgium on the basis of coat color, texture, and length (Groenendael, Laekenois, Malinois, and Tervueren), have worked as livestock guardians for centuries. They are gorgeous, high-powered, quick, and protective. With the Malinois, double the aggression and cut the gorgeous in half. Choose a Belgian mix only if its mongrel lineage includes a Basset, a Mastiff, or something else very, very calm.

The Blue Heeler–Doberman Pinscher Mix

Introducing the Bluberman. This spawn of the Blue Heeler, which went into making the athletic Australian Cattle Dog, and the Doberman Pinscher should be used only by licensed operators. Ultra-athleticism, power, speed, determination.

Sarah Wilson

Gracie

Their motto: you only herd the ones you love. A Border Collie mix may be a better, calmer pet than the purebred, as any mixing will move the Border mania down a notch. Still, expect a ton too much dog for average household use.

The Border Collie–Australian Shepherd Mix

Question: Are you prepared to take on the responsibility of another very intelligent, very demanding child? An aspiring Frisbee dog trainer may offer you his firstborn child for your dog.

When he begins a task he will finish it, whether finding lost people or figuring out how the refrigerator door opens. Like a genie in a bottle, an awesome force if you can contain it.

The Border Collie–Kelpie Mix

The Borderline Collie. Wow! Eight cylinders on a go-cart. Don't adopt this Ferrari if you want a wood-paneled station wagon. Fast, responsive, possibly dangerous. Great potential for a true pro owner with serious, important canine work in mind.

The Border Collie Mix

Brilliant, hyper, intense, restless, hyper. Did we say hyper? Border Collie genes boost horsepower of anything they mix with. Lots of folks wanted one after *The Intelligence of Dogs* ranked them the smartest dog in the universe. Sorry, adopting one as a household pet is often a mistake. Borders are brilliant thanks to a working mutt principle—they were selected for generations for function, not looks. But lacking serious (i.e., farm) work, Border Collies vibrate like fido tuning forks, herding children, cats, aunts, uncles, neighbors, everything in sight.

The Border Collie–Labrador Retriever Mix

Blending these two Type-A, Most-Likely-to-Succeed dogs is like shaking a bottle of seltzer with the cap on. A potentially wonderful all-around mutt. Like traditional concepts of God, he will seem omnipresent. See the Collie-Lab mix, and add 120 horsepower.

The Collie–German Shepherd Mix

Lassie meets Rin Tin Tin. The greatest dog on the planet, if you believe what you see on TV, and the reality can be close to the storyline. In the best of both worlds, these are superior dogs of intelligence, devotion, trainability, and protectiveness. At their worst, they combine the stupidity of modern Collies with the neurotic qualities of some German Shepherds.

The Collie–Golden Retriever Mix

Valley Girl weds Forrest Gump. Cotton candy alert. Sugary-sweet, fluffy, and not too bright, although can function as a lovable family dog who tries very hard. If you're lucky, this herding-retrieving mix, like our dog Daisy, could combine the Collie's boss-scout smarts with Golden sweetness and great Frisbee skills. If you're not, well, hybrid vigor can be fickle.

The Collie–Labrador Retriever Mix

The Collie-Lab. A winning combination of herding and retrieving skills, the Collie-Lab is a potentially tremendous mutt who will entertain family members and treat them like a flock.

The Collie X Dog

Just as every short-haired mystery dog in your local animal shelter is classified as a Shepherd X, every long-haired indescribable pooch is called a Collie X, denoting some-kind-of-Collie-cross-don't-ask-us, or Collie-Shepherd X. Many of these Collie X sightings are false. As mutts work their way, through multiple liaisons and illicit affairs, back to the Original Dog, we don't recognize the medium-size critter for what it is, a dog as nature intended. A feral package of the original dog ABCs, not the Collie X.

The German Shepherd Mix

In every dog shelter there are so many cage cards that say Shepherd X, for Shepherd cross, it's like reading the *Shepherd X Files*. True, German Shepherds have been popular for so many years that the sun never sets on mixed-breed Shepherd genes. But many of these mystery mutts are not Shepherd Xs but Feral Dog types. We see the forty-five pound dog, plus or minus ten pounds, with narrow snout, erect ears, and saber tail and we fail to recognize the mutt God keeps remaking when we let dogs be dogs. It's not the Shepherd X, it's Everydog. Tends to be very healthy, smart, sweet, adoptable. God can't be wrong.

The German Shepherd–Golden Retriever Mix

Rin Tin Grin. A world-class dog that you can find at an astonishing bargain price in an animal shelter near you: the Golden sweetens up the German, and the Shepherd sharpens up the Golden. You hope.

The Old English Sheepdog Mix

Walt Disney-isn't-reality warning: this fluffy, cuddly mix could be trouble. Disney's *The Shaggy Dog* movie led to a terrible popularity that cost this breed a lot in temperament and health. A good one is a fine pet but a lot of grooming work. A sound English mix could contain a sight hound, such as a Greyhound, or a nice spaniel. Something with good hips and a nice temperament to balance out the star-crossed shaggy dog.

The Shetland Sheepdog–English Setter Mix

The friendly, rugged English Setter with the glamorous, busy-busy-busy Shetland Sheepdog (Sheltie) spells an impressive mutt you'd want in your family. Add possible Husky influences, perhaps a long-ago romp with a randy Australian Shepherd, and you've got a dog you want on your side in a tough spot, as is the case with the remarkable Maggie in this chapter.

Samantha

The Welsh Corgi Mix

Queen Elizabeth II no doubt often says, in the privacy of her chambers, "I prefer Corgis to princesses." The Welsh Corgi (comes in a Cardigan model as well as the queen's beloved Pembroke) is a cattle-herding heart in a Dudley Moore body. This is very much a real dog, she's just, well . . . "corgi" is Welsh for "tiny dog." Intelligent, trainable, oddball-cute, she was bred little, low, and determined to drive cattle without getting kicked in the head. Some Corgis strangely suffered a canine equivalent of the autoimmune "Boy in the Bubble" disease, but geneticists have eradicated it in the dogs. Basketball fans, think Tiny Archibald, a swift, compact, muscular point guard. A Corgi double helix is a welcome addition to any gene pool party.

🐾 Ditto: Oklahoma's Littlest Hero

Neither humans nor purebred dogs could find the last victims of the Oklahoma bombing, buried in the debris of the Alfred P. Murrah Federal Building.

Not swarms of federal agents. Not technicians armed with fiber-optic listening equipment. Not highly trained rescue German Shepherds and Labrador Retrievers.

This was a job for Ditto.

Enter Elaine Sawtell, fifty, a Springfield, Missouri, court reporter, grandmother, and longtime dog lover, and her remarkable mutt, Ditto. Ditto provokes wonder wherever she goes. She is a classic Doberman Pinscher except for the half that is an Australian Cattle Dog, or Blue Heeler, which explains the white speckles on her nose and toes.

"A Bluberman is what she is," Sawtell says proudly. "It's hard to imagine a dog more athletic than a Blue Heeler with the speed and sweetness of a Doberman, but Ditto is both. Although she looks pretty weird, I admit."

Ditto wears an orange blazer bedecked with medals and title befitting a cabinet official. She is the Federal Emergency Management Agency's Canine Search Specialist assigned to the Lincoln, Nebraska, Fire Department's Urban Search and Rescue Task Force No. 1.

"That's what they call us both, actually," Sawtell says. "Canine Search Specialists. She's the canine."

Of the more than one hundred rescue dogs on FEMA teams nationwide, Ditto is one of only twelve who has attained the highest federal standards for search and rescue. (The eleven other elite Canine Search Specialists are Shepherds, Labs, and Goldens; Ditto is the only mutt.) Ditto also had the ability, rare even among top rescue dogs, to find dead bodies. "Cadaver searching," it's called.

Another way to put it is "top federal rescue mutt," Sawtell says.

In July 1993 near Springfield, a fourteen-year-old water-skiier lost an arm when she was run over by a drunken, hit-and-run boater. The next day, riding in a small boat on Table

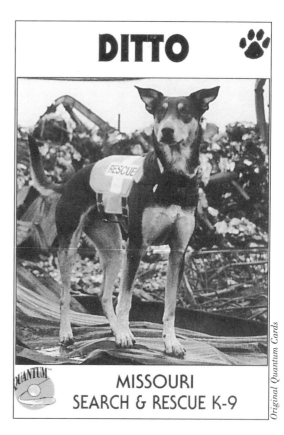

DITTO 🐾

MISSOURI SEARCH & RESCUE K-9

Original Quantum Cards

HOW THE BLUBERMAN CAME TO BE

The Doberman Pinscher, developed around 1890 in Germany, is prized for its agility, courage, and ability to steal your heart. The Australian Cattle Dog, or Blue Heeler, was bred of wild Dingos and blue merle Highland Collies to work cattle in nineteenth-century Australia. The Bluberman was identified in June 1991 near Springfield, Missouri, to the great surprise of the farm wife, when her Australian Cattle Dog bitch birthed a litter of what looked like Doberman Pinschers. Suspicions naturally pointed to the "big ol' Doberman" lazing around the farm next door. "I know I have a purebred Bluberman because I met both parents," said Elaine Sawtell, who went next door to pet the Doberman and check his teeth before adopting Ditto, the Bluberman puppy.

The Bluberman combines the fierce work ethic of the Australian Cattle Dog with the affectionate nature of the Doberman. "They want to do what you want to do," says Sawtell. "If you want to play Frisbee, they want to play Frisbee. If you want to search for cadavers, they want to search for cadavers. It's a good mix. I wouldn't have done it myself. But it works."

Rock Lake, which has 370 miles of shoreline, Ditto indicated the location of the arm in thirty-four feet of water. Divers found it twelve feet from where the dog had pointed, and Ditto became a local hero. "Ditto got a hamburger and an ice cream cone that day," Sawtell says.

On May 4, 1995, in Oklahoma City, the purebred shepherds and other rescue dogs weren't agile enough to navigate the tangle of debris, metal desks, and collapsed pillars to locate the last of the 168 bodies crushed in the April 19 bombing.

Sawtell led Ditto into the basement, into which all nine floors of the building had collapsed. The job seemed impossible. The roar and fumes of excavating machinery, the shouts of federal agents, the scent of eleven bodies recently removed hung in the stale air.

"There were so many distractions. I asked her to block it all out, to cadaver-search. It was a very confusing scent picture," Sawtell says. Yet Ditto went right to work, sniffing

slowly, methodically, combing a fifty-yard area between two collapsed pillars.

Twenty-five minutes later, near one of the pillars, she began to scratch and bite at the earth. "I was so proud," Sawtell said. "With all that commotion she focused in and made just the classic cadaver alert." Fire department teams excavated and confirmed the last three victims, where the top federal rescue mutt had indicated they would be.

Grieving families could be alerted, a chapter in a national tragedy closed, thanks to Ditto.

The next day, at the memorial service for the rescue workers, Ditto and Sawtell were asked to represent all the Canine Search Specialists who had worked for weeks in Oklahoma City.

At the service, Ditto wore her orange blazer with FEMA shield and a new button, "Oklahoma's Littlest Hero." Sawtell, who had kept her emotions in check in the basement, wept openly. Ditto moved closer to lean against Sawtell's leg, to lick her owner's hand.

"The service was tough," Sawtell remembers, "but Ditto knows me. She was so responsive to my emotions. She always is.

"That's the Doberman in her."

 Rusty

Bunchers.

They're the modern-day version of the cockney cretins who stole 101 Dalmatians for Cruella De Vil's coat. They're the clean-cut young men who answer your "Free to Good Home" ad—then sell your faithful fido to the medical lab. They're the frauds in the world of trusting best friends, the shadowy thugs who steal pets off the streets and out of yards.

One day, perhaps in northern California, exactly where isn't known, they got Rusty. They kenneled him in Oregon, dog No. 850, put a price on his head. Then Rusty got lucky: the feds busted D&T Kennels in the town of Lebanon; the owner was the first American to go to federal prison for fraudulently selling pets for medical research.

Rusty was taken to the Oregon Humane Society, where his luck continued. The shelter promised not to euthanize any of the twenty-two D&T Kennels cases. The rest of Rusty's fate was up to him.

The day Rusty arrived at the Humane Society, Andrea Wall happened to be spending her first hours as a volunteer there. Did we say Rusty was lucky?

It was April 6, 1992, the day Andrea says she laid eyes on "the most beautiful dog I'd ever seen in my life." The big red one, No. 850.

She brought him home. "The first night, Rusty walked in the house, lifted his leg on my husband's recliner, and ate all our wedding pictures." Andrea realized this was a Serious Dog. A Border Collie, only bigger, mixed with one of the few dogs that's even more

intense, an Australian Kelpie. A worker who'd make John Calvin look lazy, if you could just figure out what clock he should be punching. Anyone else might've taken Rusty back to the pound; Andrea took him on a job search.

Sheep herding? Rusty was too intense. He ran the sheep right at Andrea. Andrea, who is an occupational therapist, brought Rusty to work, where he faces the difficult challenges of helping give disabled people a second chance.

Gently shaking paws with old folks in wheelchairs, using a feather touch so his claws won't scratch their frail skin? Jumping through a hoop held by a delighted eighty-year-old woman who doesn't even realize she's stretching her injured shoulder? Bringing hope to stroke patients who couldn't bend over to tie their shoes until they got help from Andrea and her big red dog?

Why, Rusty does those things just fine.

Sue Sullivan

Rusty

 **Kismet**

According to *Webster's New World Dictionary*, kismet simply means "fate." For Mary Fox, it also means "there are no coincidences."

It was August 7, 1989—Mary's birthday, and four months since she had reluctantly put her first dog, Walnut, to sleep. "Returning home from dinner, I had a message from my therapist: was I ready for another dog? If so, she had one for me. Not sensing any urgency, I waited until our next session, where I learned to my disappointment that the dog had found a home. Ah well! It wasn't meant to be."

So Mary left for a business trip, "still a dog widow," but shopped for some dog biscuits for some mutts she knew back home. "Little did I know then why I had *really* bought those biscuits.

"What a surprise when I returned home! Not only was there a message from my therapist—did I still want the dog?—but there was urgency as well."

Mary called the dog's owner right away. "I thought I had found a home for her," the woman explained. "Today, my kids discovered the people using her as bait to teach a Pit Bull how to fight. So the kids dognapped her. If the people learn I have this dog, I don't know what they'll do."

The woman added: "She's a mutt. She looks kind of like a German Shepherd but, honestly, I think she looks like a little coyote. You have to take her right away."

Kismet has the longest ears the Lord ever put on a dog, loves tunafish, chewing gum, and skateboards, flunked obedience school, tried to kick Mary out of bed, throws temper tantrums, understands over fifty words, chases boats. "So why in heaven's name do I keep her?" Mary says.

"She came into my life on my birthday. It is surely fate."

Kismet *Mary Fox*

Important questions preoccupying Americans at this time in our history are contained in the fan mail addressed to Murray, dog star of NBC's *Mad About You:*

What kind of dog is he, anyway? Where did Murray come from?

The sanitized studio answer is: Collie mix. Adopted from a shelter. Real name Maui, like the island. "It's a rags-to-riches tale," says his trainer, Betty Linn. End of story.

But unknown to his adoring public, Murray's lineage closely resembles that of the Barrymores, Fondas, Douglases, and Sheens: he's a member of a genuine American performing dynasty.

"His mom and dad were movie stars, too," says Linn.

Murray is, however, as far as we can determine, the only multigenerational Hollywood star whose entire family came from an animal shelter.

Murray's mother, Bingo, was rescued from the Castaic Animal Shelter north of Los Angeles and went on to play the title role of the 1991 dog comedy *Bingo.* (Bingo is a "scuzzbucket mutt"-turned-circus-"Poodle" who escapes a pet shop fire, an evil Wisconsin sausage-maker, from prison by digging a tunnel, and rescues a boy by performing the Heimlich maneuver.)

Murray played backup to his mom in *Bingo* in scenes where the young son's special talent, "taking a hike," was required.

Murray

Tristar Television

"He lifted his leg on something," Linn says proudly.

Murray's dad, Max, also was a shelter rescue, Linn says. "His father is a movie star too," Linn says, "but offhand I don't remember his work."

Murray's big break came on *Mad About You,* in which he plays the devoted-but-dimwitted pet of the Buchmans, Paul (Paul Reiser) and Jamie (Helen Hunt).

Murray's dumb-dog role—he's always chasing mice into the wall—doesn't do justice to this remarkably intelligent, sensitive dog, Linn says.

Nowadays, Murray is branching out, following his mom and dad into the movies. In the film *The Good Old Boys,* he "lifts his leg," Linn notes. He also has a part in *Airheads:* a woman throws a tape out on the street and Murray walks up and, yes, takes a hike. It's his best trick.

"Tricks are easy for Murray," Linn says. "The hardest thing to get him to do on *Mad About You* is to just be their dog, relaxed, not looking at me, not looking at the camera."

So there you have it, America (thousands of his fans want to know): What does it mean for Murray to star in a sitcom?

Sit. Come.

🐕 The Saving of Maggie

She was young and running wild in a Colorado mountain town, hunting in the tall grasses around the lake, stealing from the kills of coyotes. She resembled a coyote herself, encountering humans with flattened ears and bared teeth.

"But her soft brown eyes were not the eyes of a coyote," says Jean Kenefick. "Her eyes were those of an abandoned dog, frightened and alone, searching for someone—anyone—to love her."

Night after night, the critter snuck kibbles from the plastic dish Jean set out for her. Finally she grew bold enough to approach the dish during the day. Then one morning, Jean held out kibbles in an outstretched hand. The wild dog inched forward slowly on her belly, freckled muzzle gently claiming the morsels from a human hand.

"Suddenly she was all over me; whimpering, licking, trembling at my touch," Jean remembers. "At that moment she found what she had been searching for, and she became a dog named Maggie."

Maggie and Molly

Jean E. Kenefick

The following spring Jean was walking through misty rain around the lake when a vicious, 160-pound white guard dog, escaped from a neighbor's pen, attacked. A dog named Maggie, a mere fifty pounds, flew at the White Dog's throat, and was crushed with a series of swift and brutal fang punctures into her flanks. The attack dog sniffed the fallen, bloodied body of Maggie and trotted away, sparing Jean.

"It took weeks of medical treatment and daily care to heal Maggie's infected wounds and battered body, but her courageous spirit sustained her," Jean says. "As her body grew stronger, so too did the love and trust in her eyes. Maggie has earned her place in our home, and in our hearts. Her soft brown eyes are those of a dog who knows she belongs and is very much loved."

 Soaring Sam

Sam is an ol' black-and-white mutt with graying muzzle, thirty-eight pounds, eight years old. Not nippin' at those Uniroyals like he used to. Gary Suzuki, thirty-one, is a graphic artist in Covina, California, who likes to throw a Frisbee.

"People think Sam is old and blind," Gary says, "until I take out the Frisbee bag." Then Sam becomes Soaring Sam, leaping fifteen feet off Gary's back, sprinting ninety yards to

Long Photography/ALPO dog food

Soaring Sam

nab a touchdown pass during halftime at Anaheim Stadium, as only a two-time Canine Frisbee World Champion can do. Soaring Sam, star of Letterman and Regis and Kathie Lee. Immortal, sure as a Saluki painted on Tut's tomb.

Gary is humbled by his dog. "Sam's strength is his unbelievable consistency. He has this incredible drive and I don't know what to call it, ego. He *will not* drop a Frisbee. That and the fact he gets up for big competitions, struts around like Charles Barkley, intimidating the other dogs. He's the star. He makes me look good."

Soaring Sam was created in a fusion of hyperkinetic Australian Shepherd and mega-athletic Australian Cattle Dog, which is something like splitting the atom and should not be tried at home. Gary picked up Sam one day from a local newspaper ad, like Ma and Pa Kent picked up the boy who one day landed on their farm from Krypton. Superboy had blue hair, Soaring Sam a blue fleck in one eye. Psycho Sushi, Sam's purebred Australian Shepherd sister, keeps her distance.

"The great thing about this sport is that a lot of past champions, most of the competitors, are mixed breeds," Gary says. "There's no breed bias in this sport. From all the dogs I've had, mixed breeds have been the best, the healthiest, the most intelligent. I'm a big believer that great dogs in the pound are wasting away. I wanted to win with a mixed breed. But Sam is definitely one of a kind. I don't think any dog in the sport has his abilities."

If Gary doesn't unzip the Frisbee bag fast enough, Sam unzips it and starts tossing Frisbees at Gary.

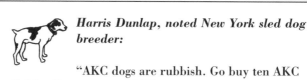

Harris Dunlap, noted New York sled dog breeder:

"AKC dogs are rubbish. Go buy ten AKC Golden Retrievers, and I'll go adopt ten dogs out of the pound, and my mutts will live longer, be healthier, and *destroy* your goldens in a dog sled race."

Human Society of Broward County

Brandi and Caroline

🐕 The All-American Spokesmutt

Talk about unappreciated mothers. Brandi, a six-year-old Collie mix, was the faithful pet of a family in Broward County, Florida. But when she had puppies, the family took her to the animal shelter with all her puppies except one, which they kept.

"What Brandi's family didn't realize is that Brandi was heartbroken!" said Caroline Crane, education director at the Humane Society of Broward County. "Each day Brandi would wait eagerly at the front of her cage, sure that her family would come back for her."

One by one all of Brandi's puppies were adopted, and Brandi was alone in her cage. "She became very depressed," Caroline said. "Brandi retreated to the back of her cage, and would curl up into a ball as tiny as she could and start trembling. Eventually, she didn't even bother to eat. Her situation was becoming serious."

Caroline, who is responsible for promoting the adoption of adult animals at the shelter, took Brandi on television to help her find a new home.

"I took Brandi out of her cage and she immediately clung to my side; I brought her

into the van to take her to the studio and she nestled real close to me, hiding her head in my lap. Once we arrived at the studio she had nothing to do with anyone else, only me! Boy, I felt special! During the entire program Brandi sat facing me with her head on my lap. The crew laughed and said I should adopt her."

Alas, Caroline had no plans of adopting a dog. "When we returned to the shelter, I had to play the villain and return her to her cage. But Brandi barked at the front of the cage, begging me not to leave . . . I had fallen in love, I adopted her!"

A year later, Brandi works as the Humane Society's official mascot. Together they have visited 120 schools, where Brandi works promoting adopting "The All-American Mutt."

At the schools Brandi tells the children not all of her friends at the Humane Society have happy endings, and pleads with them to make a lifetime commitment to their pets. Finally she opens Brandi's Pet Suitcase, Caroline explains, with everything needed to keep happy, healthy pets.

"The suitcase contains nutritional food, water, collar, tags, leash, toys, my shirt—Brandi likes to sleep on it because it smells like me," Caroline writes, "as well as a pooper-scooper, brush, flea shampoo, treats, bones, syringe/heartworm pills, and the most important thing of all—a big, red stuffed heart representing love."

At the end of the class, "children who were petrified of dogs before want to hug and love her," Caroline says. "Brandi seems so happy to feel so wanted, and I'm so proud of her. She's my All-American mutt."

🐕 Gracie, the White Dog

"Gracie's mother was a Border Collie," says her human, Cathy Atkins, "and her father was a traveling salesman." When Gracie was adopted and given to Cathy as a gift by her husband, Cathy gave Gracie a birthday—December 22, 1986, her grandparents' wedding anniversary.

Her grandparents had been married for over sixty years; Cathy wasn't so lucky. While she was in law school, in a new city with no friends, her husband filed for divorce, "surprising me beyond belief. I was devastated and didn't even want to get out of bed," Cathy remembers. "Gracie lay next to me, licking me, and just slept next to me for the first few days. She did silly things to make me laugh. As the days went on and she thought I had moped around enough, she got tough with me. She made me get out of bed by annoying me. She got me through those horrible days."

Later, when Cathy injured her back seriously in a car accident, she came home from the hospital to find Gracie waiting like a nurse. Gracie lay at the end of the bed, never coming near Cathy's back, although curling up there had been her favorite place to

sleep. "One day, deciding I had recuperated long enough, she got next to my back and half fell, half rolled into me. After that, she slept in her usual spot.

"My husband could not have known just how precious his gift would be," Cathy says. "I may well owe Gracie my life given all that happened to me during the past few years and how she helped me."

Gracie

Coat of a
Kerry Blue
Terrier.

Raised rear
of a Chesa-
peake Bay
Retriever.

Tail of a Flat-
coated Retriever.

Mystery Dog

Beard of a
Bouvier des
Flanders.

Heart—
100% Dog.

Belly of a
Beagle.

The Non-Sporting and Mystery Mutts

Mystery mutts are, at their best, the best a dog can be: incredibly friendly, smart, healthy, loyal, kind, brave, playful, and always adorable. They lower blood pressure, predict storms, save and extend lives, keep families happy. They are, in a word, dogs.

What type of dogs they are *exactly*, of course, no human can be sure. A mystery mutt is a Retriever-Shepherd-Doberman-Collie—and that doesn't explain his tail. His mother was a Golden Retriever who traced her genetic purity to the 1835 Stud Book of Lord Tweedmouth at Inverness-shire, Scotland, until it happened that night; his father was a traveling salesman. Several affairs later, such a dog's offspring could rise to one of the highest forms of canine life: the mutt beyond human powers of classification.

If you own one of these indescribable creatures, ignore the quizzical looks of passersby and puff your chest in pride. These are the most authentic dogs on the planet. Just the tonic for a late-twentieth-century world that mourns the loss of nature, individual freedom, authenticity, and diversity. The Natural Dogs. The Original Dogs. Dogs as nature intended them. Dogs as all dogs would be if we stopped arranging their marriages. Thirty-five to forty-five pounds, short-haired, thin-nosed, healthy, smart (or sometimes completely otherwise, depending on the depth of the mystery). Dogs living and breeding by their own lights.

As Joyce Kilmer might have said, had it occurred to him, "I think that I shall never see / A mixed-breed dog lovely as thee / Purebreds are made by fools to strut / But only God can make a mutt."

In this group we also make a home for those lost-soul dogs, spawns of the pure-bred Bulldog, Dalmatian, and the Poodles and others who are mysteriously classified by the American Kennel Club for what they are not as Non-Sporting Dogs.

They have nothing to prove to us as they join the ultimate mutt category. Meet now the dog's dogs. The mutt's mutts. The mystery mutts.

Descriptions and Standards of the Non-Sporting and Mystery Mutt

The Bichon Frise Mix

A nice mix to own, a Poodle-type charmer with fewer psychiatric problems. Bichon Frise means, in French, "curly-haired lapdog." You may lose in the mix some of the outrageous, cumulous-cloud-on-four-feet look that so appealed to Goya and noblewomen across the ages. But you'll likely get a good-attitude family dog. A very ambitious Bichon leaving the lounge with a very compliant Golden Retriever would produce one remarkable dog.

The Boston Terrier Mix

Friendly, lively, with a mini-Bulldog look, "The American Gentleman" of the dog world has fallen in popularity. Who, however, could resist adopting a Boston Terrier–Small Piebald Dog cross—a Boston Cream Pie.

Fritzy

Mrs. William Otto

The Bulldog Mix

Pity this charming, comical, macho mascot of the University of Georgia, Yale University, and the U.S. Marines. Created to be the epitome of strength and vitality, the Bulldog suffers just about every health problem known to dog. Ready for retirement to Arizona or Florida. A pet insurer's nightmare. The poster pup of the ravages of breeding for fad and fashion. The good news: if you find a Bulldog mix in the animal shelter, odds are she'll be a mighty good dog. A Bulldog mixed with anything improves the Bulldog.

The Chow Chow Mix

Ow! Commonly known as the Chow, which is short for what some of them wish to turn you into: dinner. Sadly, accursed popularity has taken its toll. There are some wonderful Chows out there assembled by careful breeders, but these are not the dogs allowed to run loose unneutered and create Chow mix love puppies. Some aggressive, unpredictable Chows have contributed their genes to the mixed-breed pool, meaning be especially careful around Chow mixes. They can inherit a tendency to give little warning and no quarter.

The Chow Chow–Shar-pei Mix

If you find one, present it to your worst enemy. Say, "I'm sorry I insulted you last week. I got you a gift. I'd like to mend fences . . . here's a puppy." The puppy will already be gnawing fingers, like the cute T-Rex infant in *Jurassic Park*. This mix of two breeds plagued by health and temperament problems will almost certainly be trouble. Don't take this pup home from the pound.

The Dalmatian Mix

Don't expect spots. Random breeding tends to erase them. That makes this mix hard to, uh, spot, unless you've met the mother and father. Call these mixes Dalmotions—expect ceaseless motion, guarding instincts, and hair on the carpet 365 days a year except leap years. The Dalmatian mix hails from a coach guardian breed made to run many miles a day. Without daily aerobic fitness challenges, your Dalmotion likely will misbehave.

The Golden Retriever– Blank–Doberman– Blank–Shepherd Mix

You fill in the blanks. Whatever it is, Stu and Maria Bykofsky of Philadelphia have one. (To decide for yourself, see the picture on page 125.) Says Stu: "Her mother was yellow, probably a Golden Retriever mix, mixed perhaps with a Shepherd. We admire Shepherds, so we hope so. Puppy build and markings suggested Rottweiler, but as she grew she stretched out into what appears to be a Doberman. There's no question she's a retriever too because she always retrieves objects nonstop. Her ears don't hang down like a Beagle's, or up like a Shepherd's, but are broken in the middle. To us they look like little butterflies. But we may be taking poetic license."

The Husky-Collie Mix

The loving owners of Licorice, whose story of suffering and redemption is told in this chapter, assured us in writing that Licorice was, in their words, a "Husky-Collie???" After close examination of Licorice's history, we concur. He is certainly a Husky-Collie???

The Husky–Dalmatian–White German Shepherd Mix

Dakota, the incredibly sweet dog who appears in this chapter to be absolutely insane, is an Australian Shepherd–Dingo mix, its owners say. We love Dakota, but this is not likely. There are not many Dingos in suburban United States. Dakota's ears are too big for Aussie or Dingo blood. Perhaps a Husky–Dalmatian–White Shepherd mix. Perhaps some Australian Cattle Dog. Perhaps.

The Junkyard Dog

The proverbial type. Guardian instincts. The Junkyard Dog in this chapter had the mythic origins typical of this type, born under a junked car, fed milk from an old hubcap. Otherwise, who knows? This mutt might as well have come out of a cloud, like Zeus. The ancients knew that life is enriched by humbling mysteries. Consider your life enriched.

The Keeshond Mix

The "Shepherd-Collie mix" you adopt from the pound could easily be a Keeshond-Labrador mix. Yes, another mutt mystery further deepened by knowledge. Keeshond crosses should be all-around nice guys, true to the "Dutch Barge Dog" form that kept them popular in the Netherlands for two centuries. A little barky but trainable and eager to please.

The Little Tan Dog

Here's how to determine if you have one of these very sweet and easily recognizable dogs, such as Eddie, pictured in this chapter. Eddie most definitely is a Sight Hound–Labrador mix, with the coloration, the strong cheek muscling, the narrow nose, and whopping muscle in the back of the thigh. Then he sits up and appears to thicken, meaning he is most certainly a Pit Bull–Labrador mix. Then he starts to run and allows us to triangulate the question to its finest point. We have determined beyond a reasonable doubt that Eddie is a dog. A Little Tan Dog.

The Poodle Mix

When choosing a Poodle mix, remember this has been one of the world's most popular dogs for decades, meaning there are Poodle crosses everywhere. A good Poodle mix has intelligence, style, playfulness, famous charm, some guarding instincts, and is one of the best dogs in the world. A poor Poodle brings to any mix an unhelpful serving of neuroses, yappiness, the attention span of a gnat, and the brain pan of one besides. Poodles can be evalu-

Sarah Wilson

ated by the Poodle Sanity/Size ratio: the taller the poodle, the more sane; the smaller the dog, the less so. Look for mixes that make the poodle calmer. Just about any dog may make some poodles calmer. You won't find anything sweeter than a poodle.

The Shar-pei Mix

Warning: this mongrel may need time to get its act together. In 1978 *The Guinness Book of Records* named the Shar-pei, the Chinese dog whose name translates to "draping sandpaper-like skin," the world's rarest dog. Alas, it was once rare in the center on the Eastern food table. Exotic reports spawned interest and popularity and now the Shar-pei is a pet everywhere. Another breed plagued with health problems and questionable temperament. Proceed with caution with mixes.

The Small Piebald Dog

Take the genes of the *Our Gang* dog, Pete, whisk the mix thirty times, and let set. This is what you get. One such mutt, Trixie, became a Ken-L Ration Hero Dog. About Trixie's lineage we can say with total confidence in our scientific method that one fine and loyal heart met another and created a third.

The Yellow Dog

Like Radar, the remarkable yellow mutt whose story is told in this chapter, the classic Yellow Dog is a Labrador Retriever–Chihuahua–Basenji–Great Dane mix. Any four unrelated breeds mixed together turn out approximately like this, a feral dog type with yellow influences. Mix four breeds, however, who have very similar body types, like the Rottweiler, Rhodesian Ridgeback, Pit Bull, and Boxer, and you get a melting-pot version of a Pitty-Rotty-type dog. (See the R2B2 mix in the Working Mutts chapter.)

Sarah Wilson

Hurricane Andrew destroyed their home in the country and forced them to relocate to a small apartment in a Miami suburb. Jim and Sherry Norris and their son, Scott, six, took a few boxes of belongings and their two mutts, Gipper and Cindy.

Shortly after moving back into their rebuilt home, Sherry opened the front door to see why the dogs were barking—and saw a yellow shape dash across the street into the rejuvenating mango grove.

For several months the elusive stray was seen roaming the neighborhood fields. Scott spotted him one morning sunning in the middle of the road and said he looked more like a fox than a dog.

One October evening, Sherry was walking the fields marveling at the restored grove—and there, in the moonlight, stood the stray Yellow Dog. "He froze as I walked slowly toward him," Sherry says. "I saw how pitifully thin he was. His huge ears were alert, tail curled over his back, hair straight up on his neck. I stopped and softly called to him. He turned and ran across the street. The next morning the Yellow Dog watched from his burrow as we went to school."

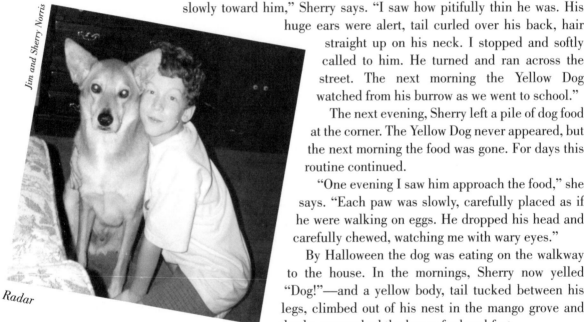

Jim and Sherry Norris

Radar

The next evening, Sherry left a pile of dog food at the corner. The Yellow Dog never appeared, but the next morning the food was gone. For days this routine continued.

"One evening I saw him approach the food," she says. "Each paw was slowly, carefully placed as if he were walking on eggs. He dropped his head and carefully chewed, watching me with wary eyes."

By Halloween the dog was eating on the walkway to the house. In the mornings, Sherry now yelled "Dog!"—and a yellow body, tail tucked between his legs, climbed out of his nest in the mango grove and slowly approached the house for breakfast.

"After months of feeding him we named him Radar. Before long Radar responded to his name. He looked less emaciated. His tail stayed tucked between his legs, but he was growing bolder.

"One November evening," Sherry says, "he reached out and put his paw on my hand. He watched as I stroked his offered limb. A few days later I could pet his head.

"Soon Radar 'knocked' whenever he wanted to come into the house. Jim invoked the no-more-dogs edict and I promised to do something about Radar's future.

"I enlisted a neighbor to help me load him in the van for a trip to the veterinarian.

With a clean bill of health and legally registered in Dade County it was time for a newspaper advertisement: Free to good home large, neutered male dog. Very sweet, needs a loving family.

"Scott couldn't understand why Radar couldn't stay with us. We pointed out we had two dogs, Radar wouldn't stay in our yard, and daddy didn't like all the escape holes he dug. Radar had to go to a new family. Logical as it seemed to my husband and me, our child saw only the love he felt for the dog.

"A family came to our house to meet Radar in December. The mom, dad, and teenage daughter said he was a handsome dog, and my heart sank when they said they would take him. As they backed down the driveway his black nose was pressed against the window and his eyes watched as Scott waved goodbye. The three of us walked back inside, adults silently telling themselves it was for the best, child heading sadly to his room. It was a very quiet Friday night.

"Sunday morning their call came. He had escaped when the family had gone shopping for an hour. He'd used a bush to scale the five-foot wall that surrounded their home. I was horrified. Their home was approximately fifteen miles from us.

"City and county roads and the Florida Turnpike separated our areas. We knew what he was trying to do—come home. I was sick. My first impulse was to hop in the van and join the search. But I didn't want Scott to see the probable outcome, a dead dog. The guilt was immense. My poor little boy spent all day outside playing on the front lawn waiting for his friend to come home. I waited for the inevitable phone call to say that he had been found injured or dead.

"Five o'clock and still no word. I called them. They'd searched and driven around but could not find him. Dade County Animal Control was closed until Monday.

"Monday arrived with the weekday routine: dress, fix coffee, wake Scott for school. Jim wanted the sports page; I'd forgotten to bring in the newspaper. As the garage door slowly grinded open I gasped—there in front of the door was our damp, lost dog. I yelled, 'He's back, he's back, Radar's back!' He trotted into the kitchen. Jim and Scott ran down the hall and hugs, licks, and a furiously wagging-tail frenzy erupted. Then he drank a bowl of water, wolfed down a bowl of food, and collapsed on the floor. The van drove itself to school that day. Our Christmas miracle really happened!

"Radar is a treasured family member now. In the morning he fills my vacated spot in bed, his head on my pillow. Since he has been a house dog his coat has turned to a beautiful shade of gold. He is forever our golden mutt."

 **Dakota**

There's somebody, we're told growing up, for everybody.

This was not the case with Dakota, the deaf Dingo-Aussie mix. He was in and out of shelters for most of his one and a half years. Perhaps because Dingos were implicated (falsely) in stealing a baby in the Meryl Streep movie *A Cry in the Dark*. Perhaps because Dakota had crazier blue eyes than Gary Gilmore. Perhaps because he was deaf.

But when Dakota appeared on a Denver TV news show as Friday's pup, Stephanie Welpton fell hard and fast for the deaf spotted cur with the wacky eyes and bit-off ear. She began volunteering at the shelter every week so she could visit him. When Dakota's playmate was adopted, Stephanie couldn't bear to watch Dakota so depressed. She took him home.

The savage Dingo mix, it turns out, "loves his family and friends more than food," graduated at the top of his obedience class, plays hide-and-seek, buries his bones in the laundry bag, and "touches the heart of everyone he meets," Stephanie says.

The savage Dingo mix, as far as we can see, is actually a Dalmatian-Husky-Something. (The odds of your mutt being related to a dingo is about the same as the odds of you being related to Henry VIII.) Not that any of this matters.

"He is my most wonderful mutt," she says. "Not only do we forget that he is deaf, we forget that other dogs can hear."

Dakota

Stephanie Welpton

🐕 Cheech & Wrong

Three young men promised Mary Callahan they would take fine care of her family dog, Duke, who wasn't allowed in the Callahans' new condo.

Instead, the young men taped the Dalmatian's mouth shut and tied him to a tree, then sicced their Pit Bull on him. While Duke was still alive, his ears and tail were cut off, his belly sliced open, his throat slit. Death came, finally, as the dog's skull was crushed with a cinder block.

Philadelphia Daily News columnist Stu Bykofsky had the car radio on that summer day in 1994 when he heard about Duke's death. It sickened him. Bykofsky, a gossip columnist in his fifties, is a newspaperman of the old school: gruff, streetwise, cynical.

So it was to the astonishment of his colleagues that the death of an animal moved Bykofsky to abandon his snippy items on local celebs; the gossip columnist was writing with the righteousness of an Old Testament prophet. As Duke's case went to court, he wrote: "My wife and my dog will stand outside the courthouse as silent witnesses for Duke. You can join us there, alone or with your pet."

More than seven hundred people attended the hearings. And a hundred dogs.

Day after day, Bykofsky thundered about the death of an innocent at the hands of "cretins," "monsters"; the need for justice. He inspired fifty thousand people across the United States to sign petitions demanding jail time and psychiatric counseling for the three young men, all in their twenties. Except he did not call them young men. "The three dirtbags," as Bykofsky put it, "the degenerates who committed the outrage." The dirtbags drew some of the harshest terms in history for animal cruelty—up to three years in jail.

Bob Laaramie

Cheech

"It was the barbaric nature of the crime that got me," Bykofsky said. "People said to me, 'It's only a dog.' But that's not the point. It was cruelty beyond comprehension. And it deserved to be answered."

Bykofsky answered it, leaving his readers to wonder: What softened the heart of this hard-bitten man?

A year before Duke's death, Bykofsky and his wife, Maria, had adopted a homely

mutt, Cheech. It was Bykofsky's first dog since the mutt Lucky, whom Bykofsky had as a boy growing up in a small Bronx apartment. Lucky, like Duke, couldn't follow his family to their larger apartment in a city housing project. "If I think about this thirty-seven years later, I cry," Bykofsky says. "Excluding the deaths of my grandparents, giving up Lucky was the saddest moment of our family's life."

Lucky's successor is Cheech, a Retriever–Doberman–Shepherd–Shih Tzu mix. Cheech, saved at the eleventh hour from execution in the animal shelter, lives the good life nowadays. It's not uncommon for Maria Bykofsky to serve her husband chicken, while Cheech gets ground sirloin sautéed with grated carrot and garlic, with a side of rice.

"I'm Jewish and Maria's Italian so Cheech gets treats on both Hanukkah and Christmas," Bykofsky said. "Cheech has two ethnic heritages in addition to Doberman."

🐕 Licorice

Licorice

John and Geri Sorensen didn't like dogs. When they visited friends, John would make his discomfort known; friends would lock their dogs out of his sight.

Then one day in May, a young couple moved in two doors down with a mongrel named Licorice. The couple said they'd saved the dog from an abusive home. Licorice got his name because he kissed everyone.

So John and Geri were surprised when Licorice's new owners shackled him to a four-foot chain attached to a doghouse, punishment for digging. Then they moved the doghouse to a vacant lot behind their home. Licorice could barely get into his doghouse and had to practically sit in his poops. His owners worked long hours and seldom walked him, fed him irregularly, locked him in a garage when it thundered so the neighbors wouldn't hear his crying and barking. The dog whimpered pitifully when humans came near.

"Like I said I'm not a big dog lover," Geri says. But she felt she had to say something. She expressed concerns to the neighbors, but little changed. She didn't know what else to do.

Geri was agonized when Licorice had to endure the cold Wisconsin winter in a doghouse, but she felt helpless. When spring came his owners said they were moving and couldn't bring the dog. Then Geri knew exactly what to do. She and some neighbors decided to find the dog "a new, and believe me, better, home," is how Geri puts it. Weeks passed, but the neighbors couldn't find anyone interested. Meanwhile, Geri kept Licorice in her yard when she was home and moved his doghouse closer to her property to keep an eye on him.

In April, when Geri was cleaning out flower beds, Licorice "came over to where I was kneeling, put his head between my arms, looked at me with soul-searching eyes, and planted a kiss on me," Geri remembers. "I melted. How could I give this lovable creature up? How could I be certain that he would not suffer again at another's hand? I told him I would be his mom and that he would not have to worry about a home. He could live with us and I would take care of him. He seemed to understand, and had a happy look about him."

John and Geri had had cats before, but never a dog. Walks were new for all concerned. "Our arms were about pulled out of our sockets on the leash," Geri says. They took Licorice to the vet for the first time in his life, got him neutered, got him his shots. After the visit to the groomers, "We were shocked at how handsome he was under all that dirt!" Geri said. Licorice, best they could tell, was a male "Husky-Collie???" Geri writes. John agreed the new sun room should have a doggy door, and the backyard a fence so Licorice could run the yard without being tied up.

"I cry when I think of his past neglect," Geri says, "but our pets are always spoiled. We treat them as children because my husband and I were not able to have children. People often tell me that if there were reincarnation, that they would like to come back as one of my pets.

"If you are lucky, you will get a mutt someday like my Licorice," Geri adds. "I guess we are all lucky we found each other."

🐕 The Junkyard Dog

Ralph Salerno was working in an auto salvage yard when a female dog wandered onto the yard and "sort of took over like she was our watchdog." No one knew where she came from but she stayed. She accepted food, but shied from being petted. The men noticed her bulging stomach. "We called her the Ma Ma dog," Ralph said.

One day, the boss's young son was playing near the junk cars when he found a litter of puppies under a car hood lying on the ground. Ma Ma kept moving her pups, but Ralph kept a close watch and always found them again.

Soon Ralph noticed one of the pups wasn't getting enough to eat because the other pups crowded him out. "I told my wife about it and she suggested that I take milk out there and feed the little guy. So I did!"

Ralph Salerno

Boots

Ralph mixed powdered milk in an old hubcap and fed the runt. Soon the rest of them got some too. When the pups were six weeks old, Ralph recounts, all found homes with the men "except the one I had been feeding powdered milk to.

"It was about Easter that I took that little guy home and gave him to my wife," Ralph says. "I said: 'We're home. I hope you like him. Don't worry, he won't get very big.' "

Of course, he was huge. His name was Boots because of the markings on his feet. Everywhere they went, Ralph said, "This is Mr. Boots, my Junkyard Dog." He was a good watchdog and slept on the bed at Ralph's feet. He never got sick, except he got shot once when he strayed a couple of blocks from home at night. "We had to take him to the vet's and have BBs removed from his backside," Ralph remembers.

As time went by, Boots couldn't jump up on the bed anymore, and slept on the rug next to Ralph's side. Hip dysplasia got so bad Ralph had to put Boots to sleep. The old junkman man held him fast, and wept while the vet used the needle.

"Boots lived with me more than fifteen years and a day does not pass that I don't think of him," Ralph says. "I never felt for any animal like I did for Boots. I loved Mr. Boots, my Junkyard Dog."

🐕 Eddie, the Little Tan Dog (Two-Time Loser Wins)

Eddie was the kind of dog who faces the longest odds: a two-time loser. Five or six years old, no spring puppy. Not so cute anymore. Two different owners had given up on him, bringing him back to the Champaign County Humane Society in Illinois.

Eddie's chances at a third adoption looked grim. One problem was, most folks want to know what kind of dog they have; Eddie's cage card said, "Shepherd Cross," universal shelter language for "heck if we know."

Eddie

The rest of the card said: "Not good with children and chews on furniture." A bookie wouldn't have put good odds on Eddie.

But to Emily Snyder, age twelve, Eddie's charm was the sum of his flaws. "My mom knew he wouldn't get adopted with that cage card," Emily says. "She went home that day and begged my dad to get him."

Dad was the voice of reason, as dads often try to be. Weren't three dogs enough? Then he went for a look himself. "There were other dogs available for adoption," Edward Snyder said. "Some bigger. Many prettier. Eddie was sort of nondescript. People had trouble placing him. 'The little tan dog' was the best they could muster. But Eddie had that look in his eyes. Anyone who failed to pause long enough to look into those eyes and see the potential for love and companionship missed a treasure."

On the ride home, the dog "not good with kids" laid his head on Emily's lap. Later, Emily didn't know what to think when Eddie "wagged his tail so hard that his whole body wiggled, then he jumped on me."

It turned out the two-time loser had a serious, heretofore unrecognized, flaw: loves children too much.

Emily was worried when the dog jumped on her, but dad reassured her: "Eddie wants to drive home the point that he loves you and is afraid it won't be emphatic enough . . . so he jumps on you."

"Eddie," Edward Snyder says, "has found a permanent home where he will be loved, cared for, and cherished for as long as he lives. And beyond."

 Betty Linn, Hollywood animal trainer and trainer of Murray, the Collie mix on __Mad About You__:

"At least 95 percent of our dogs in Hollywood come from the pounds, shelters, and rescues. Even our Doberman comes from Doberman rescue. Mutts are often better to work with. Sometimes, some of the breed dogs get hyper and have lots of health problems. Mutts are just great."

🐕 Who Was That Masked Mongrel?

Every year since 1953 the Ken-L Ration dog food company has awarded a gold medal for America's Dog Hero of the Year. America was a much different place in 1953: all dogs apparently were Collies and German Shepherds. Thus the contest favored pure-breds with names like Lassie, who in 1956 awakened a California family to alert them to their young son's hemorrhaging after a tonsilectomy. Or Dutchess, a noble German Shepherd who in 1958 watched his family's sailboat overturn in a Minnesota lake and dove in to save the day.

By 1971, you could have renamed it the "Lassie and Rin Tin Tin Memorial Award." Of the eighteen hero dogs who had been recognized, only three were mongrels—and even they were Collie or Shepherd mixes.

That year, Trixie broke the mold. In truth, Trixie, a chubby little thing with a wide white body, a narrow black raccoon mask and tan cheeks, broke the mold being born. In 1971 Trixie became only the fourth mongrel to win the Ken-L Ration Hero Dog award.

Heinz Pet Products

Trixie

But the judges awarded her an extra distinction—the first hero dog "whose ancestry was a complete mystery." Indecipherable mutt though she may be, the judges concluded, there was no doubt this was a dog. And a dog "of extraordinary intelligence."

Adopted from an animal shelter for $5 in 1968, Trixie led a quiet life as the pet of the Richard Sherry family of Lynn, Massachusetts. Then one cold spring day, two-year-old Ricky Sherry, unseen except by Trixie, squirmed through an opening in the fence that enclosed the Sherrys' backyard. Trixie followed the tyke.

The water of Buchanan Bridge Pond stood at 35 degrees that day. The youngster somehow lost his footing on the bank and fell into the frigid depths.

After a while, people started looking for Ricky. Mrs. Felix Manna, a next-door neighbor, was among those searching for him when she encountered Trixie, sopping wet and barking like mad. She followed the dog across backyards and fields to the water's edge, where Trixie resumed her crazed barking. The woman looked through the mists but saw nothing.

Trixie, seeing her message wasn't being understood, leapt into the icy water, paddled out a short distance, and began swimming in a small circle, barking all the while. Staring intensely at the center of the circle, Mrs. Manna finally perceived the tip of the child's aqua-colored jacket, which blended perfectly with the water. She plunged in and brought the child out.

Firemen responding quickly forced "unbelievable amounts of water" out of the child's lungs, but found no signs of life. Ricky was dead. At Lynn Hospital, doctors who had lost hope detected a faint heartbeat, the first in twenty minutes, and Ricky was miraculously revived. Medical history was made when he subsequently recovered without the slightest mental or physical damage.

Little Ricky was allowed to return home to Trixie, who ran in happy circles, barking like crazy.

PART THREE

Selecting and Training Your Random-Bred Dog

Dakota and Stephanie

SELECTING A MUTT

Selecting a mutt is like selecting a favorite color—there are endless possibilities! Often, when a mutt is a straight mixture of two breeds, the physical and behavioral tendencies of both parents are clearly visible. With many of America's dogs though, the whole is indeed greater than the sum of the parts. Nonetheless, understanding the history and common behaviors of the main ingredients of your unique magnificent mix will give you valuable insights into her character.

Purebred dogs were originally created to perform tasks—herd cattle, locate food, pull sleds, kill vermin, guard property, and otherwise make themselves useful. Each of these tasks required a special dog selected for generations for specific behaviors and a body type that made performing these tasks possible. For example, no one would mistake a Chihuahua for an Arctic sled dog. Nor would you think a Chow, with his heavy coat and squat build, would make an ideal desert hunter. The work these breeds were created to do still influences their behavior.

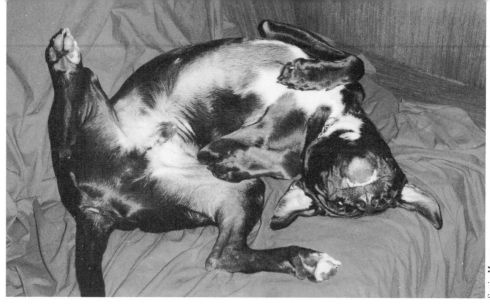

Hobbs

Sonia Moyer

The Sporting Mutt

THE POINTER MIXES

Brittany, German Shorthaired, Vizsla, Weimaraner

Pointers run fast and hard for many miles looking for game. Once the quarry is located the dog locks into a point, holding that point until the hunter catches up.

What to Expect

A strong-minded dog who thinks for himself. While not uncaring about your desires, his instincts often take precedence. Athletic in every ounce of his being, if not exercised a great deal—an hour or more a day when young—he may redirect that energy into activities you do not find amusing, such as chewing, hyperactivity, or jumping.

THE RETRIEVER MIXES

Curly Coated, Flat Coated, Golden, Labrador

Created to work closely with man, taking direction carefully, even at long distances, these dogs are extremely trainable. Used extensively as guide dogs for the blind and as all kinds of service dogs. At their best, these are some of the best brains and biggest hearts in the canine world.

On the downside, their popularity has led to widespread health and, tragically, aggression problems. We never saw a bit-

ing Golden Retriever until the mid-1980s. Now they are sadly commonplace in our training work.

Like spaniels, there are less common retrievers who have been spared the price of popularity, but it would be extremely unusual to find a mix with Curly Coated Retriever heritage.

What to Expect

Because retrievers are some of the most popular dogs around, their mixes are plentiful. Normally you'll find a happy, loving dog who is athletic, exuberant, and kind—occasionally to the point of being goofy.

Their sins fall into the category of over-enthusiasm. Leaping up to say hello, dragging you down the street to see another dog, stealing food from the counter. They have been bred for centuries to retrieve, so they are normally oral. Most retriever mixes will chew in their first year or two. A crate (see Crate Training later in this chapter) and long-wearing toys are a retriever mix's best friend until they get a little older and wiser. Obedience training gives them the direction and manners their enthusiastic personalities need.

Einstein: Before . . .

. . . and After

Patrick Harrington

THE SETTER MIXES

English, Gordon, Irish

Setters are also bred to range far looking for birds, but as a group they tend to be a bit softer-spirited than some of the pointers.

What to Expect

The three setters recognized by the AKC are as different from each other at this point as apples and oranges. In light of this, we will deal with them individually.

Irish setters can have, to put it gently, a high activity level. To say this is like saying that an elephant is a little large. Some of these elegant animals also have the attention span of gnats. Run them hard, train them patiently, and don't lose your temper—that will just confuse them.

Gordon Setters are handsome, normally friendly dogs. What some may lack in problem-solving skills they more than make up for with a goofy kind of charm. The rarest of the setters.

English Setters are a nice breed of dogs; normally not too hyper, with a good brain. Gentle, loving—if you have an English Setter mix chances are you have a nice dog.

THE SPANIEL MIXES

American, Clumber, Cocker, English Springer, Field

These charming little dogs were created to run about near the hunter and flush game into the air within range of the gun. They worked with man and because of that are, at their best, trainable and owner-sensitive.

What to Expect

Purebred American Cockers and English Springers are a sad tale of the price of popularity. Decades of being two of America's favorite purebreds have led to some poor specimens and the general demise of these two wonderful breeds. However, some of the basic charms of these dogs can still be seen in the many mixes that exist.

The best spaniel mixes are sweet, adorable, charming, devoted, and generally loving, lovable dogs. Common spaniel problems that may crop up are submissive urination (they urinate when nervous or excited), chronic ear problems, and, most sadly, aggression. Both English Springer Spaniels and American Cocker Spaniels nowadays have serious aggression problems.

There are other spaniel breeds that do not suffer from these problems to the same extent, if at all—English Cockers, Sussex, Field to name a few—but a mix from one of them is extremely rare.

The Hound Mutt

THE SIGHT HOUND MIXES

Afghan, Greyhound, Saluki, Whippet

Before guns, man needed an extremely swift dog to run down game for him, so man created the sight hound. These dogs, once they have a moving object in sight, will pursue it until they have it or can't see it anymore. Usually, they run quietly.

What to Expect

Consummate couch potatoes and seekers-of-comfort: buy a well-stuffed dog bed or resign yourself to sharing the couch with your mix. These dogs should never be let off lead in an unfenced area. Even when you think they are safe, you'll be amazed at the large amount of ground they can cover so quickly. And, although these are some of the more elegant dogs in the dog world, do not mistake this for their being wimps. These can be predatory animals around smaller animals and some can be aggressive toward people if surprised or intruded upon.

THE SCENT HOUND MIXES

Basset, Beagle, Bloodhound, Coon Hound, Foxhound

Scent hounds have a nasal autopilot. They put their noses to the ground and go, not

Jedediah

Jana de Peyer, Best Friends Animal Sanctuary

thinking about anything else until they come to the end of the trail. All this while barking so the slow-footed humans can locate them.

What to Expect

These animals are friendly, gregarious, and generally good-natured. Predictably single-minded when it comes to smells. Their obsession with odors translates into garbage eating both from the can and à la carte off the street. Unless properly fenced, their nose may lead them astray.

You can use this inbred focus to your advantage by training with treats. Get the attention of this group's nose and you have them. Barking when bored, excited, frustrated, or left alone is another common trait. And, in some cases, difficulty in housebreaking.

The Working Mutt

THE FLOCK-GUARDING MIXES

Anatolian Shepherd, Great Pyreneese, Komondor, Kuvasze

Big, beautiful white hulks of dogs that look peaceful but are ready to spring to the aid of any of their family, should they perceive a need. With the exception of some of the Great Pyrenees, who have been much softened by years of breeding for show, these dogs are not for first-time dog owners. Naturally suspicious, independent thinking combined with a willingness to be aggressive, these dogs are generally not for novices.

What to Expect

Lots of training! You need to get these dogs used to the idea that you actually are the leader and worth listening to. Extensive, ongoing socialization with all kinds of people and animals is mandatory. Expect adults of these mixes to be fairly laid-back most of the time until they perceive a threat, like a ringing doorbell. Then they will spring to life with a vigor and determination that will surprise anyone who doesn't know their history.

THE GENTLE GIANT MIXES

Bernese Mountain Dog, Newfoundland, Saint Bernard

This category covers a range of tasks from water rescue to pulling carts. These dogs are huge and, as a group, nice dogs. Normally easygoing, accepting of events and people. Their size makes them prone to short lives and health problems.

What to Expect

Normally pleasant dogs that fit in well with many families. Although usually tolerant of well-behaved children and other animals, early training is mandatory because of their size. Even common misbehaviors such as jumping can be downright dangerous if a one-hundred-pound-plus-dog does them. Some of these breeds drool, but mixes are less likely to. Lots of hair all round. Their only real drawback is the bigger the dog, the shorter their life. Truly giant dogs are often lucky to see ten years of age.

THE NORDIC MIXES

Alaskan Malamute, Samoyed, Siberian Husky

Meet the sled dogs. Partners in the north, these dogs made survival in the harsh icy climates possible. They served as trans-

portation, guards, herding dogs, and hunting companions. Predictably, given their environment, these are tough dogs—physically and mentally.

What to Expect

Active, playful, strong-willed, and magnificent, these dogs, like terriers, have their own following. People who love Nordic dogs seem to want nothing else in their lives. Because of their history, expect heavy shedding twice a year and moderate shedding the rest of the time. Many of these dogs have a great sense of humor, which may seem like an odd thing to say until you've known one. Crate-train your Nordic mix because a bored Nordic can be a destructive Nordic. Many Nordic breeds were hunting partners, so some of these mixes may be predatory. Early socialization and training can help moderate this.

THE PROPERTY- AND PEOPLE-GUARDING MIXES

Akita, Doberman, Great Dane, Giant Schnauzer, Rottweiler

Large, powerful dogs created with the ability and desire to protect if they feel that it is needed. Which, by the by, is not always a direct match to when *you* feel it's needed.

Many of these breeds have been purposely softened by their breeders but still enough are out there to characterize these breeds as handfuls who need experienced, dedicated handlers to reach their full potential as dependable family members.

What to Expect

Drive, focus, commitment are all typical traits of these crosses. They want to be with you every second, doing something that's important. If you don't give them things to do, they'll make things up. One guard breed mix I know has made it her mission in life to keep all the other dogs in her household away from the family cat. The cat doesn't seem to notice, but the dog takes the task seriously.

Not all guard breed games are so innocent. Continuous training and constant supervision are key. A special note here on training methods: we do not ever support rough methods and some guard breed mutts will teach you why themselves. These dogs have been selected over the centuries for a willingness to respond to aggression with aggression. We know of a few instances where guard breed dogs have bitten their owners and, *in most cases,* the owners attacked the dogs first. Keep the words *leadership* and *partnership* firmly in mind when training these dogs.

McFly

Liz Sharpe

The Terrier Mutt

Australian, Border, Cairn, Norwich, Scottish

Before effective poisons, complicated traps, and metal-lined storage containers there was a huge rodent problem on farms. This huge problem needed a huge answer and that answer came in the form of small dogs with big attitudes. Terriers were created to kill vermin of all types, which they did with startling efficiency. Some of these dogs were also developed to fight other dogs as well as larger prey like foxes, badgers, and bears.

What to Expect

A fun, impulsive, opinionated, charming, tough little dog who will, if necessary, take on the world. Terriers have been selected to respond to attack with attack, so don't try to win through intimidation.

Unless socialized with other animals and trained effectively, some terrier mixes can be predatory and/or dog fighters. The thing to remember about terrier mixes is that they may well enjoy a good fight, entering into the fray with a wagging tail. Think of them like the old cowboys in movies who joined the brawl with a smile on their faces. Such behavior must be controlled and such dogs must be on lead or in a safe fenced area 100 percent of the time.

Sitka

Here we recount a tale for which we have no explanation. Make of it what you will.

Sitka had a litter of puppies: the biggest, fattest one was named Huggy Bear. Huggy Bear was a favorite of the family he was born into. It was not a hard decision to keep him.

One day, their owner got ready to go out to a meeting. As so often happens in New York, she was running late, rushing to get out the door. She bid farewell to the pair and hurried off, down the four flights of stairs, out the heavy, double doors, and down the street. Several blocks away from home, the owner stopped. She heard something. She felt something. It was Sitka, crying in distress. How could it be? No windows in her apartment were open and even if they were, how could she hear the little dog so many blocks from home in a noisy city like New York?

Already late, she stood torn for a moment, then rushed home. Now she simply had to check. Back the blocks she raced, up the four flights, through the door to find Huggy Bear wedged behind the old steam radiator in the living room. The wall was marked where Sitka had tried in vain to free him. Both of them had copious diarrhea, they were so panicked. The radiator had come on, and was heating up terribly. Those old ones would burn you if you touched them; they would have tortured poor little Huggy Bear, maybe even killed him.

It took the owner a few minutes to turn the radiator off and pry Huggy Bear free. She does not know to this day how Sitka called her. What she does know for sure is that there was no way to hear her screaming from so many blocks away. What do you think happened?

Sitka

Hope Ryden

Bozo and Ninon

Bozo was not exactly the dog Ninon went looking for. In her mind's eye was a sweet, doe-eyed female, all tail wags and soft licks. Maybe maturing to fifty pounds tops—an easy size to travel with and she wouldn't be able to pull too hard on the lead. With all this resolve, Ninon went to the shelter.

Amidst all the barking dogs begging for attention stood a huge, serious-eyed dog in the gangly stage of growth. The card on the cage said Keeshond-Shepherd cross but he was already too big to fit that bill.

This hulk of a dog had been there for many days; his time was running out. The voice of a friend came back to her. He had urged her to take a risk, try something new. She had thought this meant indulging in her long-denied desire to get a dog. Now she knew it hadn't. It had meant this dog. This big, powerful beast of a dog. Something about him grabbed her, and it hasn't ever let go.

Intellectually, Ninon knew he wasn't the wisest choice. But her heart gave her no option. Trying to hold on to a small part of sensibleness, she inquired if a dog could be returned if it didn't work out. The woman at the front desk assured her yes, of course. With that, a great friendship was born.

Dubbed Bozo in an effort to make him seem less threatening to the people she lived with, he came home. Like all new couples, they had a few things to iron out. His past owners hadn't ever discussed manners with him and he leapt up on her a lot—especially when her back was turned. He thought he was a lapdog, trying awkwardly and unsuccessfully to climb up for a cuddle. He dashed through the open door, only to be returned by a kind, bologna-toting neighbor. But they worked it out, as love, time, and determination often can. At this writing he is eight years old, much beloved, and inseparable from the woman who saved him.

Bozo and Ninon

Sarah Wilson

The Toy Mutt

Maltes, Papillon, Pekingese, Pug, Shih Tzu

These man-made little tidbits of dogs exist solely to please us.

What to Expect

Charming, bossy, demanding, intelligent, and too cute for words are descriptions that fit many a toy mix. The mutts we've met are utterly adorable. Toy breed problems are largely owner-caused; the list includes faulty housebreaking, aggression, barking, demanding attention, finicky eating, refusing to walk on lead, climbing on the furniture, and ripping up paper. Treating them like real dogs instead of tiny little playthings will eliminate most of this list.

Muffin

Bonnie Packert and Fred Watkins

The Herding Mutt

Australian Cattle Dog, Australian Shepherd, Border Collie, German Shepherd

Brilliant dogs! Can be annoying dogs because of that intelligence. Ever been with a toddler in the question-asking stage? "Why is the sky blue?" "What was that noise?" "Where does smoke go?" Herding breed mixes are the same way. "What are you doing?" "Can I help?" "What's in the closet?" "Should those kids be playing that roughly?"

Active, involved, persistent, directed, protective, and sensitive (this less so for the cattle-herding dogs in the group), these crosses are both rewarding and demanding.

What to Expect

A lot. Get active with your dog. Jog, participate in agility and competition obedience activities, teach tricks, play flyball, or all of them at once! These dogs need work, they crave work, and they will make you crazy without work. These are not dogs you can leave at home all day, and then expect them to hang out by the couch at night and not develop alternative entertainments like spinning in circles while barking, herding the neighborhood kids into the garage, opening the refrigerator, or taking up the linoleum one piece at a time. These are great dogs—willing and wonderful—but they don't tolerate boredom well.

The Non-Sporting and Mystery Mutt

Non-Sporting is the catchall category of the American Kennel Club. All kinds of dogs, with a wide range of original purposes, end up here. Rare breeds are virtually any breed not recognized by the AKC—which are hundreds worldwide.

Each dog's original purpose must be understood to understand the breed's influence on your mixed breed. For example: Dalmatians would fall into the working group. Bred for running along under and guarding horse-drawn coaches, this breed would add athleticism, endurance, and a strong watchdog ability to the mix. They may also add epic shedding.

What to Expect

Read up on the breed's individual history, then extrapolate the impact it might have on the unique combination canine at your feet.

Seumas: Before . . .

. . . and After.

Newell Dunlap

Sarah Wilson

Adult Dog Evaluation and Selection

The adult dog is the much overlooked option in acquiring a new companion. Several unfounded myths about older dogs will be dispelled here.

Myth No. 1: An older dog won't bond like a puppy. FALSE. Many older dogs bond quickly and completely to their new owners, quite often becoming more devoted than many mutts raised from puppyhood in the same home.

Myth No. 2: They will be more difficult than a puppy. FALSE. Anyone who believes this obviously hasn't raised a puppy lately! A new addition to the family will take some time, no matter what the age or species. Older dogs, with their normally lower energy level, full bladder control, and all their adult teeth, often settle in quicker and with less damage to the home than puppies.

Male Versus Female

This is a personal choice. Once dogs are neutered, the sex differences in temperament are greatly reduced. Each individual animal is unique. Despite the fact that many male dogs are more pushy, directed, with more aggressive tendencies than females, two of the sweetest-natured, most tolerant dogs we have ever owned have been neutered males.

On the female side of things, they are rumored to be softer, easier to deal with, and less assertive. Yet two of the most directed, strong-willed dogs we have owned have been females. So, generalizations aside, go by your own preference and the individual traits of a specific dog.

Hope Ryden

The Importance of Looks

It is human to imagine what your perfect dog looks like, to want a dog of a certain color, size, or shape, but in the long run none of that really matters. What is important is how easy the dog is to live with, how kind he is to children, how playful he is or active or whatever it is you value in a companion. Don't get hung up on a fantasy. Choose the dog with a temperament that matches yours and you will fall wildly in love with his looks.

Myth No. 3: Old dogs can't learn new tricks. FALSE. Older mutts of unknown history are routinely adopted from shelters by law enforcement and service dog institutions. Dogs for the deaf, narcotics-sniffing dogs, arson-detecting dogs, and more were all someone else's throwaway. Older dogs learn brilliantly: don't let that silly old myth stop you!

The next section explains a few ways you can evaluate the older dog you are considering.

WITH THE FAMILY

There are many reasons why a family gives up a beloved dog. They might be moving, their working or financial situation could have changed, a family member may be ill—the list is long.

There is a longer list, though, for people who voluntarily elect to give a dog away and these are the situations you need to screen carefully. A dog who is out of control, a nuisance, or aggressive is frequently a candidate for "getting rid of."

You want a pet, not a problem, so trust your gut instinct about a dog.

When you arrive at the dog's home, is he indoors or out? Indoors is a better sign. Check the backyard for a chain, pen, or doghouse. Dogs raised mostly outdoors rarely make as good a family companion as dogs raised inside with their people.

Is he friendly or standoffish with you?

Friendly is a nice signal, though I would not condemn a dog for being uninterested; after all, he has no idea who you are yet. Some barking at the door is to be expected, but growling, snarling, stiff, slow movement, or staring at you in a hard way are unacceptable.

Is he friendly or standoffish with his people?

A dog who seems unattached to his own family is a bad bet. Some breeds are more aloof than others and here's where your own preferences come in. If you like a dog who doesn't fawn all over you constantly, then a distant attitude may be perfect.

Nancy Ward

Riddle, a Pointer Border Collie cross, looks a bit gangly here, but he grew into a beautiful, cherished companion.

How to Read a "Free to a Good Home" Ad

"Room to Run"
This standard refrain usually means the dog is inadequately exercised for his needs. People are sometimes unprepared for the normal exuberance of canine youth. Without a productive outlet, many dogs become a pain in the neck to live with. This is not their fault. They may well become the model mutt with appropriate exercise, training, and confinement.

Other "Room to Run" dogs have been chained in the backyard for long periods. These dogs—especially if isolated during the critical puppyhood months—are not good candidates for adoption. Through no fault of their own, these mixes may be hard to housebreak, overly territorial, and a challenge to manage in the house.

Unless you are up for the task, leave adopting these animals to experienced dog handlers. This is not a simple project. Yes, it is sad and a waste, but there are literally millions of charming mixes out there who need you just as much and who will integrate more easily into your family.

"Older Children Only"
These dogs are either overly exuberant with small children or aggressive. Find out which. Such behavior is often due to mismanagement, but never dismiss or underestimate signs of aggression. Aggressive dogs can be managed, rarely cured. We do not recommend adopting aggressive animals unless you are experienced and successful with this type of dog. Most shelters avoid placing such animals for adoption.

"No Cats/No Other Dogs"
Read here: chases and may attack other animals. If you are planning a single-dog household with no other pets, this problem can be worked with. Plan for a sturdy fence and no off-leash time outside that fence until you get some professional assistance.

More than one dog who is perceived to be aggressive with other animals is actually just frustrated, bored, and/or mishandled. With guidance, these animals can calm themselves right down. Proper direction and training are key here. You must get the help of a qualified trainer or behaviorist.

Ask about what he likes and doesn't like.

Be open and friendly, because you want the people to be open and friendly right back. If you ask them straight out "Does the dog bite?" you may not get a completely honest answer. If you chat with them, you'll have better luck. Ask them what kinds of things the dog dislikes. If they are not forthcoming, ask them about toenail clipping or going to the vet. Almost every dog dislikes these things. Confide that your last dog hated these things; that may make them feel more comfortable about giving you the real dirt, if there is any. Then ask what he does when he doesn't like something. Inquire about what kinds of situations make him aggressive. You want all the cards on the table.

Ask what commands he knows and have them show you.

A trained dog is a valued dog. People who have taken the time to work with their dog are usually more committed owners than people who haven't. People who valued the dog are more likely to have cared for him properly.

How upset do the people seem?

If someone is telling you that they have to give up their dog for health or job reasons, yet doesn't seem the least bit upset about it, something is fishy. Beloved dogs will be missed and that should show.

If the person answers all your questions quickly and with positive answers (Yup, great dog. No problems at all. Loves kids, the mailman, and even my Aunt Millie. Washes the car. Makes omelets for us on the weekend . . .), you may be getting a snow job. Be careful.

Do you see toys, a dog bed, bowls, a lead and collar?

It is a good sign if people have spent some money on the dog. Again, it points to the dog being valued, which is promising.

Is the dog neutered?

Neutering is another investment. People who make that investment often value their pet's health and well-being highly. If the animal is not neutered, ask why.

This older shepherd/golden mix pup would make a great selection for a family with children.

NOT WITH THE FAMILY

Dogs in a shelter, found on the street, or at your local veterinarian cannot be assessed as above. Such a dog has many unknowns, and some behaviors, both good and not so good, may not present themselves until the dog has settled into his new home. Starting immediately with positive training and direction can stop many unwanted behaviors before they begin.

Regardless of this, here are a few things to look for and avoid when considering these companions.

Cage Behavior

Squat down in front of the cage so you face to the side of the cage, not directly at it, and speak in a kind way to the dog. Offer your hand outside the cage: no fingers through the bars, please.

GOOD

Reactions we like to see range from sitting quietly and watching you to enthusiastically offering to greet you back, paws up on the wire, tail wagging a mile a minute.

(continued on page 154)

Neglect: Case Study

The Crowleys didn't start out planning to neglect their dog. They had great plans for their new companion. Dad had a little extra time in his weekend, he was going to start jogging with the dog. Mom didn't mind the extra work; she kind of liked having the dog around when her husband traveled. Even little Janey had big plans: she was going to teach him tricks. So off they went and adopted an adorable Terrier Plus Who-Knows-What from the local shelter. Janey named him Scamp.

Dad did make a few halfhearted attempts at jogging but he never really liked to so he soon stopped. Mom didn't quite realize how much extra work a puppy was and soon found it easier just to tie Scamp outside. Housebreaking never completely happened, basic manners like not jumping up or stealing food or leaping on the couch never were taught. Instead of teaching the dog what they wanted him to do, they told him "No." And "No" became the word he heard most and understood least. Soon the Crowleys found it simpler just to put him outside.

Janey loved Scamp but as he got bigger he knocked her over in his enthusiasm and that took all of hers away. She kept her distance from him.

Besides barking when outside, the puppy still grew into an adult, he still ate and drank, and the Crowleys didn't think much about it. That is until the neighbor started complaining about the noise. Then, not knowing what else to do, the Crowleys took Scamp back to the shelter where surely some other loving family who "had more time" would adopt him.

Dogs take time. Time to train, exercise, play with, and love. They take money for vaccinations, training, food, equipment, and toys. Puppies take more time. They enter the world knowing only dog things—to nip, to leap, to pee wherever they please. It takes time and tolerance to teach them otherwise. For us dog lovers it is a burden we seldom ever feel but it is a burden nonetheless and if you aren't ready for it, if you think you're getting Lassie in a mutt outfit you will probably be disappointed and the dog will end up paying the price.

There is not a long line of people who want a grown dog with no manners, who isn't housebroken, who chews destructively, and is generally unruly. If you can't stand the dog, what makes you think someone else will? Do the basic work of manners and commands. This animal is trusting you with his life, don't blow it.

RECLAMATION

Fortunately, old dogs can learn new tricks. It may take a little longer to undo a bad habit than form a good one, but it can be done and is done thousands of times a year by dedicated adopted dog owners everywhere.

Tie Her to You

The first thing a mutt with this history needs is to bond to you. One of the fastest ways to form that bond is to put the dog on lead and keep her with you. In the house, in the yard, whenever you can, simply have the dog tag along. A few days of this and you'll see wonderful changes in your new companion's opinion of you.

Crate-Train

When you can't have her on lead with you, confine her. Not only will this prevent bad habits from surfacing but it gives the dog a needed sense of security as well. Please see the box on Crate Training for detailed instruction.

Play Training

Lighthearted teaching is needed here. The more the dog learns, the more relaxed, attached, and secure she will become. It doesn't much matter what she learns—tricks, commands, whatever—just teach her! The exception is no aggressive games, please!

Constant Supervision

In the room with you or crated are the only two indoor options until this dog is settled in. Keep the same level of supervision on her as you would a toddler. You wouldn't leave a toddler by herself while you take a shower, would you? Then don't leave this dog. Prevention not only is a major key to changing bad habits, it is also the easiest part. Don't skip it!

Plenty of Exercise

Universally, the more exercise a dog gets the better behaved he is. Time invested in a good romp twice a day is time well spent.

Time spent exercising your pup is never wasted.

Heartstring Heartache

Every year boxes of these free pups get hauled around to yard sales, malls, and supermarket parking lots. In general, don't look, don't touch, and don't take. Any puppy who actually stays in a cardboard box is too young, too frightened, or too sick to take home.

Just because a puppy is weaned does not mean he is ready to be given away. Although pups can be weaned as young as three weeks, important mental and social development goes on in the litter until seven weeks. Pups taken too early from their canine family can grow up with aggression problems—both to dogs and toward people. Development missed in those first few weeks can never be replaced.

AVOID

Dogs cowering in the back of their cage, any type of snarl, growl, or teeth baring, turning away from you, barking at you nonstop, or flinging themselves at the wire in a state of near hysteria. Of course, any of these dogs may well be the next Wonder Dog but the odds are not in your favor.

On-Leash Behavior

The ideal place to do this is in a quiet, separate room, but this is not always possible. If a room is not available, improvise. A hallway, bathroom, or secluded spot outside might work. Ask the shelter personnel for their help.

Have someone take the dog out of the cage on lead. Depending on the dog's size, at a distance of a few feet squat or bend down, speak kindly to her, and observe what happens.

GOOD

This is hard because many dogs are simply overwhelmed by the situation, spending much time nose to the ground trying to investigate everything. This is fine, give these dogs a few minutes to search about, then make another overture. We like a dog to show interest in you at some point.

During either the cage introduction or the on-leash time, a dog may urinate a bit when you greet her. A quick small squirt or two is quite polite and appropriate. It is a frightening situation, so give the dog some leeway here.

A dog who lets loose the next Great Flood may have been trying to hold it in her cage and should not be penalized for being well-housebroken in an impossible situation. Give these dogs the benefit of the doubt and spend some more time. If they continue to urinate, however, that may be a problem.

AVOID

Dogs who continually and totally ignore you. Dogs who try to hide, cowering away from you. Dogs who leap at you nonstop in a frenzy. Jumping is to be expected in this situation, but not franticness. Jumping is easily remedied, fundamental energy level is not.

This dignified, older dog would blend gracefully into any family.

Shelley Singer

Puppy Evaluation and Selection

Puppies are hard to resist. Vulnerable, innocent, adorable imps, we are hopeless for virtually all of them. Selecting one puppy from a sea of cuteness is a challenge. That's what this section is about, sorting out the likely from the potentially difficult. In lieu of a crystal ball, the following sections should enable you to find exactly the right puppy for you.

Ideally the puppy has been with her mother and litter mates for the first seven weeks of her life. Do not take home any pup younger than five weeks or who has been taken from her litter before five weeks old. These animals simply haven't had enough time with the mother and their siblings to learn the canine ropes. What is missed in those first weeks cannot be made up for later, all too often leading to heartbreaking aggression problems later on.

Before you go to select a pup, keep in mind that there are thousands of wonderful mixed-breed pups who are waiting for you. The right match exists and is well worth looking for. With that thought firmly in mind, let us meet the pup.

WITH HER LITTER

If you are set on a certain sex, have the owner put away all the others. This way you'll have a clearer look at the ones in which you are interested. Watch the puppies interact for a few minutes. Which

How would you choose between these two adorable pups?

Caren Sage

A healthy puppy
looks and smells
clean, there is no
discharge from the
nose or eyes. Acti-
vity is normal,
listlessness is not.
(Although napping
is frequent with all
pups.) Their
surroundings
should be clean as
well. They should
be a good weight,
neither with ribs
sticking out or
with a huge,
distended sto-
mach. A big belly
on a ribby puppy
can be a sign of
worm infestation.
And lastly, a
bright eye and an
eager lick are both
good signs.

pup is curious about you? Which is head-ing off to explore? Does anyone sit by her-self and cry?

The puppy you want is friendly, re-laxed, confident, and playful. The best way to find her is to do the tests outlined at the end of this section. These will give you excellent insight into the fundamen-tal temperament of the puppy.

EVALUATING A SINGLE PUPPY

Many puppies, especially in shelters, can only be evaluated by themselves with lit-tle or no history to go on. This is how you approach assessing these dogs.

Approach the cage and speak kindly to the pup. Cowering, refusal to even look at you, or any type of aggression should re-sult in a 100 percent veto. No excuses. This is a decade or more of commitment; be sensible.

Normal responses range from wild enthusiasm to calmly sitting there watch-ing you. Wild enthusiasm is more common but there is little wrong with a pup who takes a bit of time to warm up as long as he passes the rest of the tests with flying colors.

Now take him out of his cage and, if you can, put him down in a quiet room. Many shelters now have "get acquainted" rooms for prospective dog owners and their prospective pets.

A shelter pup will likely be over-whelmed initially—either running about the room exploring or sitting quietly get-ting his bearings. Simply observe the be-havior and say nothing. A pup who walks through the center of the room repeatedly

is confident. A pup who hugs the wall or stays under a chair is nervous.

After a minute or two, clap your hands softly and call him to you. He should come. Maybe not immediately, but within a minute or so he should be with you say-ing hello. If he ignores you or shows no interest, put him back. You want a people-oriented puppy.

Here are five easy tests you can per-form on any pup to give you a good indi-cation of the inborn temperament of your potential companion.

1) People-Oriented

This puppy comes up to you and stays around you much of the time. If she goes off to play, she comes back readily when you call her kindly and squat down. Avoid all pups who refuse to approach you, show little interest in you, or can't wait to get away from you.

2) Ability to Calm Down After Stress

Pick the puppy up and gently cradle her upside down in your arms. Normal reac-tions range from lying still but relaxed to mild struggling, mixed or not with periods of rest.

Avoid all puppies who lie stiff in your arms, cling to you, who struggle hysteri-cally, or become very vocal. A few pups will even attempt to bite. Skip these pups; they will be a great deal of work with no guarantee of success.

3) Willingness to Forgive

After cradling gently put the pup on the ground, speak to her kindly, and stroke her gently. A good pup will forgive you instantly, wagging her tail, licking at your face, and generally being adorable.

If the pup leaves your side and refuses to return, skip her. Life happens, tails get stepped on accidentally, toes get pinched in doors by mistake: a dog has to forgive and forget to be a safe companion.

4) Sound Stability

When the pup is three or four feet away from you, toss a ring of keys or a training collar so it lands a foot or two behind her. A good reaction ranges from ignoring it completely to startling, then investigating. Skip any pup who startles and hides, refusing to see what happened. Noise is a part of our world, and a dog who fears it can make the Fourth of July, thunderstorms, and local construction hard on everyone.

5) Touch Stability

This is nice for any companion dog but truly critical if you have children. While holding the pup, apply pressure to the skin between her toes with your fingertips. Press down lightly at first, increase pressure until she reacts. Immediately release the pressure and play with the pup. Be careful *not* to use your fingernails. Good reaction: You apply rather firm pressure before she whines and/or pulls her foot away. Bad reaction: Pup screams at light pressure or attempts to seriously bite you. Some gentle mouthing is pretty

Through puppy testing we found that Friday would try the patience of Mother Teresa.

normal. You'll know the difference: one hurts, the other doesn't.

CHARMING PUPPIES TO AVOID

The Boldest

She runs right up to you, leaping against you nipping at your nose. She unties your shoelaces, then races off to taunt her litter mates. This type of pup can be absolutely charming—and an absolute handful in the house. This pup may be the perfect selection for a working dog but about as appropriate for your house pet as a Ferrari is for the family car.

The Shyest

Oh, this one yanks on your heartstrings. Sitting huddled by herself, she just needs a little love and she'll be perfect, right? Wrong! You want a puppy, not a project. A

shy pup is always likely to have shy tendencies, which can easily bloom into fear-based aggression. With so many happy pups just waiting to grace your home, why select an obvious problem?

The Noisiest

This one "talks" to you. You scoop her up, she chortles. You put her down, she whines to be picked up. You pick up another pup, she barks at the indignity of it all. Cute? Sure, at five pounds. But wait until she's seventy pounds. Wait until you're trying to sleep. Wait until your neighbors are trying to sleep! Most pups will be vocal at one time or another but you don't need one who never quiets down, especially if you live in the city.

Training Your Mutt

When it comes to dog training, it makes no difference whether your dog is pedigreed or a love child. What does matter is the experience a dog had before it arrives in your loving hands. Too often mutts have a "Triple A" background, meaning they've been *a*dopted, *a*bandoned, or *a*bused. In this section, we discuss the special needs of these companions, as well as some easy solutions to some of the typical problems this history can cause.

Detailed information on command training as well as a comprehensive guide to canine behavior problems can be found in Brian Kilcommons and Sarah Wilson's first book, *Good Owners, Great Dogs*, listed in the Training Resources section of the Bibliography.

ADOPTED

Many wonderful animals are adopted from shelters and individuals each year. Animals come up for adoption for two general reasons—either the family must place the dog because of a move, a divorce, or an illness or the owners want to place the dog because it is a bad match between dog and owner. Roughly translated, "bad match" means the dog is making the owner crazy, usually because of the dog's basic nature, preventable behavior problems, or a higher energy level than the owner wants.

An adorable little terrier mix we know drove his original owner crazy. This little bundle of energy barked a lot. His owner felt he barked at everything. Instead of training the dog, this first, frustrated owner got rid of him. The new owner? Adored the little energy ball. His only complaint? He wondered whether there was some way to get him to bark more!

One person's trash is another person's treasure.

Mutts honestly placed because of life conflicts can be an instant companion. Just add love plus structure and these happily adored animals will settle into your home with a sigh and a tail thump.

You may never know the whole story of the new mutt in your life, but you don't have to. His new life starts the day you bring him home. What he needs most is structure, in the form of routines, training, and confinement, and stress-release outlets, in the form of play, exercise, toys, and positive training.

Adoption: Case Study

Mayo came to Susan because she was not adapting well to the new man of the house and vice versa. Mayo, a Boxer-Samoyed mix, was a sensitive dog who had been given pretty much a free rein for the first five years of her life. Because she was a friendly, well-mannered dog, training had seemed unnecessary to her single owner, who doted on her. But when a man entered the picture Mayo did not react well. She took to urinating on his possessions and on his side of the bed. She refused to respond to his commands and taunted him by staying just out of reach. Though all of this was probably workable, he lost patience with the dog's antics. It was decided that it would be best for all concerned to find her a new, loving home. She landed with Susan, who had known the dog for years and was quite fond of her. Familiar or not, Mayo was stressed by the change. Urination mistakes increased, and she appeared depressed and withdrawn.

Luckily for her, Susan knew just what to do. Instead of babying the dog, which would have only made her worse, Susan set about treating her completely normally. By following the steps outlined below, Mayo improved immediately, becoming completely problem-free within a couple of months.

RECLAMATION

Any change of home is stressful for a dog. A change into a stranger's home is even more difficult initially. Luckily, with a little time and energy invested, your new dog can settle in, becoming a trouble-free member of your family in a relatively short amount of time.

Positive Training

The more stressed a dog is, the more leadership she needs. Positive training, which emphasizes reward for correct behavior, is the quickest way to establish your leadership, build a bond, and create an understanding between you and your dog. As an added benefit, being able to direct your dog to a positive behavior with a command is the best way to eliminate unwanted bad habits she may have arrived with.

This shy terrier mix benefits more from kind-but-sure structure than from babying.

Jim Kalett

Structure

Structure applies to all things in your new dog's life. Structure her time with predictable routines, structure her energy with appropriate exercise. Structure her thoughts with training and work. The more structure you give her in fun, fair, and firm ways, the quicker she will settle happily into her new home.

Confinement

Confinement is a part of that structuring. Until she is well settled, she needs confinement anytime you cannot have your eyes on her. Confinement means in a crate or behind a gate. Having a place that is hers and hers alone, where nothing bad ever happens, where she knows you will always return, is a gift you give her. Most adopted animals come to love their confinement areas, seeking them out on their own for naps.

Calmness

These animals do not need theatrics whenever you come and go, or babying when they show fear, or hysterics when they make a mistake. Take a breath. This is a huge change for the dog, one she did not ask for even though it may have been needed. It takes at least a month, often several, for a dog to truly adjust to her new home. During that time, be patient and stay calm; she is doing the best she can.

Play

Play is a great stress release for both you and your new companion. Play gives an outlet for excess energy, calms the mind, and bonds the two of you together. Indulge yourself daily in a romp with your dog. Some dogs will arrive at your home not knowing the first thing about play. You get the privilege of introducing it to her! What fun! Play ball, teach tricks, go for a swim. Just please avoid games that promote competition between the two of you—like tug-of-war, chase me, and keep-away. These are not productive and should be avoided.

ABANDONED

Every year many beloved canine companions wander away from home, get disoriented while at a vacation house, or make a break for parts unknown, while still others are dumped out like so much garbage.

If you find a dog, check with your local shelter for any rules or regulations that may apply. Some states require you to turn a found animal over to the shelter for a period of time, giving the owner a chance to claim him.

The first group of misplaced mutts often make wonderful companions. No matter how wonderful they are, though, do run an ad in your local newspaper saying what you've found. Don't be too specific in your ad. If you've found a friendly, huge male Newfoundland-Lab mix with a purple collar, simply state: "Found: Large Black Dog." Allow the caller to tell you the sex, hair length, collar color, and any distinct markings. This will assure you that the caller truly is the long-lost owner. Sometimes it is hard to return a happy mix to whom you have quickly grown attached, but think of it this way: if you ever lost such a companion, wouldn't you want someone to return him to you?

Animals dumped as trash are a particular tragedy. This cruelty usually occurs at the end of summer vacation or the college year. People who got dogs for short-term use dispose of them by the side of the highway, edge of a park, or anywhere they find convenient. The assumption is that somehow this protected pet will blossom instantly into a self-sufficient predator, surviving on his wits and instincts. This is about as likely as you being able to survive in the wilderness. What will happen to these animals is they will die in some slow, painful way such as by starvation, disease, injury, or poisoning. These animals—confused and betrayed—deserve another shot at the good life.

Animals dumped for behavioral reasons are often more a reflection on the dumper than the dumpee. With some basic obedience, crate training, exercise, and love many of these throwaway dogs become well-behaved, cherished members of the family.

Chloe After . . .

Chloe Before . . .

Hope Ryden

The first stop for a found mutt is the vet. Since the history of the dog is unknown, you need to take every precaution to protect his health. Animals under stress are more susceptible to disease, and even a positive stress, like coming to a new home, can set some dogs off. A common new home problem caused by the combination of stress, new food, new water, and a new life is diarrhea. Ask your vet what you can do to prevent this. Also, having your veterinarian run a fecal test for parasites can head off a problem before it develops. Use only worming medications prescribed by your vet. Over-the-counter medications are not as effec-

tive and almost any wormer can be dangerous if not given at the proper dosage.

You will want to give your new friend a rabies vaccination immediately. Your vet may well recommend other vaccinations as well as a heartworm test and preventive medication. Have a female dog checked for pregnancy. More than one mother-to-be gets dumped by her keepers who don't want the "problem" of puppies. All pet dogs should be neutered as soon as possible. Anyone who loves dogs will make sure this is done. With millions of dogs—of all ancestries—being killed every year for lack of a home, it is the least we can do for these animals we love.

 Abandoned: Case Study

Hope found Smiley at the entrance of the Queens-Midtown Tunnel. A fellow dog lover stopped as well. Together, using a looped lead, patience, and good luck they managed to get Smiley into Hope's car. Smiley was safe but still terrified.

None of us will ever know what that little dog had been through. All he could ever tell us in his own eloquent ways was that humans had never meant anything good to him. For a week he lived with Hope as an unhappy house guest. Though she tried her best to make him feel welcome, he slept under the table in a corner. He ate ravenously as if he didn't know when or where his next meal was going to come from. He accepted Hope's company to some extent, but snarled at any attempt to touch him.

Then, in the middle of the night, Hope awoke to whining. It was Smiley, whining as he paced near her bed. In a heroic act of faith he leapt up next to her, flung himself against her, giving his soul to her at that moment and for the rest of his life.

With the exception of John, Hope's husband (whom Smiley actually selected for her), no one else's touch was ever welcomed. Though he doted on Hope, becoming inseparable from her, willingly learning all manner of tricks and games, he would show every tooth in his head if a stranger's hand reached toward him.

Hope, so aptly named, redeemed our species in this little dog's eyes. And we surely needed that redemption for whatever terror and harm someone obviously inflicted on this innocent life.

RECLAMATION

This is a hard type of dog to save. In many households—ones with small children, active households with strangers in and out all the time, or inexperienced dog owners—this small dog would never have settled in and could have become a danger to himself and to his family.

If you have the experience, responsibility, lifestyle, and time for such a project, here's how we recommend going about it.

Patience

You can't rush fear. It leaves when it's ready. Attempting to force its departure tends to make it dig in its heels. Reclaiming a dog with this kind of history takes as long as it takes.

Hand Feeding

Feeding your new companion all his meals from your hand is an excellent way to gain his trust. Feel free to use a spoon if he's a grabber or you feed wet food. If the dog is especially timid, take a step back every time he takes a bite. This step back is a reward for a fearful dog, as it gives him more room; you retreat, which will relax him and allow him to approach you for the next tidbit.

Smiley

Hope Ryden

Self-Rewarding Setups

Alternatively, if your dog has taken up housekeeping under a bed or some other hiding place, you can set up meals as adventures. Before you go to bed, dole out his food on small paper plates in trails around the house. Put down food every foot or so with bigger piles being left furthest away from his hiding place. Every morning you can judge his progress by the empty paper plates. This rewards him for being adventurous as well as getting him acquainted with the rest of your home.

Positive Training

It is critical that all teaching be strictly positive with these dogs. Progress is made through guidance and reward. Shamelessly use whatever your dog enjoys to motivate him. A hug, a ball, or a raisin—as long as your dog enjoys it, use it! Make the sessions short—less than five minutes; fun—his tail should be wagging; and frequent—two to three times a day. You'll be amazed how quickly these dogs learn once they understand what you are trying to teach them.

Routine

Daily routine is a simple remedy for a frightening world. Meals at the same times, walks at the same time, a treat at bedtime—all these things make a worried dog feel less worried. The downside to this is weekends. Your dog won't understand what they are, so resign yourself to getting up early, at least for the first few months. On this same note, try not to give your friend too much extra attention on the weekends—that will just set him up for anxiety on Monday morning.

ABUSED

Mental/Emotional Abuse

Mental/emotional abuse takes many forms, but the most common are neglect, yelling, isolating, tormenting by children, and unpredictable owner behavior. Mutts who have suffered through this may exhibit a wide range of behavioral problems, including—but not limited to—destructive chewing, barking, housebreaking problems, self-chewing, shyness, possessiveness, and fear-based aggression.

To resolve a problem you must address not only the problem itself but the total environment that has created this problem. Behavior problems in abused dogs are frequently stress-release activities. Both controlling the stress in his life and releasing it productively are necessary to successfully change his behavior. These dogs desperately need reliable, unemotional direction from their new owners and tons of exercise.

Mental/Emotional Abuse: Case Study

Rowdy was well named. This exuberant Rhodesian Ridgeback–Golden Retriever mix defied gravity much of the time. His case of mental abuse is subtle and perhaps more correctly labeled mishandling, but it is so prevalent that we include it here.

First and foremost, Rowdy is adored by his owner, a single woman. They are devoted to each other. She showers him with almost constant attention. He brings her toys; she throws them. He rests his head in her lap; she strokes him for hours as she watches TV. Maggie, the owner, thinks that loving him means giving him everything he wants whenever he wants it.

As Rowdy has grown to his full seventy pounds of gleeful activity, some of his previously cute behaviors have begun to wear thin. Maggie tries to be tolerant, as she knows he means well, but sometimes when she's dressed up and he playfully tugs at her clothing or he hurts her when he leaps up, she gets angry and yells. Then, feeling guilt-ridden, and all too much like her mother, she heaps attention on him to make up for it.

Recently, Rowdy did the unthinkable and growled at Maggie when she lost her temper. He's even starting to look at her funny when she asks him to get off the couch. She gives him all the love she possibly can, how can he behave like this?

Easy. Maggie is goodhearted but misdirected. All her months of constant attention, waiting on him hand and paw have led him to believe he's the leader. When she becomes angry; especially over a behavior for which previously she praised him, like jumping, he becomes confused and frightened. This confusion increases his activity level, making more conflict inevitable. Her flip-flopping between complete indulgence and incomprehensible anger creates a perfect scenario for him to begin trying aggression.

RECLAMATION

Loving dogs means giving them what they need—which may or may not be what they immediately want. This includes sorting out what you want emotionally from what the dog actually needs; two easily confused but very different things.

Work for a Living

Rowdy is bright, active, and bored beyond belief! He needs work to do. Linking commands with things he enjoys—play, petting, food, walks—is the single best way to make commands both relevant and fun. You work hard for the things you love, why shouldn't your dog?

Please and Thank You!

Dogs may not understand words well. They may not comprehend technology, aerospace, or the information superhighway but dogs do know relationships. Every time he paws you and you throw his toy—or pet him—or give him a treat—he has given you a

command and you have obeyed. Good human! Turn the tables on him! When he paws you for something, make him say please by sitting or lying down on command. It works wonders.

Set Boundaries

The basic rules of canine boundary setting can be summed up as follows: Thou shalt not maul, mouth, or mount me! This includes, but is not limited to, pushing you out of the way at the door, leaving scratch marks down your front when you return home, leaping onto your lap from halfway across the room, or leaving tooth marks on your arm "in play." Treating you like a chew toy is not respectful. You are asking for trouble if you allow any of the above behavior.

Ignore Dog

In the world of dogs the submissive dog gives attention to the leader dog. Every time you go to your dog and attend to him you are worshipping at his altar. Now, for many dogs this never becomes a problem, but for a bossy dog it can lead straight to an aggression problem! No more than ten minutes of attention—total family attention—per hour. If this sounds hard, then you need to do it. If this sounds impossible, take up a hobby that does not involve the dog. Let her come to you for attention, then make her work for it. You'll be surprised just how effective that is.

Direction Instead of Anger

Next time you are tempted to get angry, try telling the dog what you want her to do instead. If she jumps up, command "Sit," follow through, then praise! If she gets up on the furniture, tell her "Off," use a leash and collar to guide her off, then praise! Dogs learn much quicker when shown what should be done with patience and praise instead of punished in ways they can't quite understand.

Physical Abuse

All too many people still think that the only way to "teach" an animal anything is to hurt and terrorize her. This is not teaching, it is abuse. From rubbing a dog's nose in her own mess to whacking her with a newspaper, this kind of treatment is wrong. Most human beings find themselves becoming abusive for two reasons. One, they have been told it works. Two, they don't know what else to do.

In certain cases, abuse may stop one problem but it will cause others. The fact that it does, on occasion, work is not an argument for it. Other, saner methods work better without making your dog frightened of you, your spouse angry at you, and you feel horrible.

Not knowing what else to do is what leads many people to violence. They feel that they have tried it all and still the dog is doing the wrong thing. The remedy for this is education—of yourself—not abuse of the dog. Just because you have done all you know how to do does not mean you have done all there is to do. Educate yourself. Read training books, talk to training professionals, buy training videos—the information is out there. Find it. Use it. Your dog, and you, will benefit.

Physical abuse's telltale signs are hand shyness (when you lift your hand suddenly above the dog's head as if to strike him and he cowers), hyperactivity, submissive urination, and aggression, especially if threatened.

Dogs who have never been hit are not hand-shy, although a few herding breed mixes may hit the ground at any fast motion made in their vicinity. Their tendency to flatten at fast movement is a survival skill. By lying on the ground, any kick in their direction will go harmlessly over them. Border Collie and Australian Shepherd mixes are the top candidates for this response.

When a mixed breed is fearful of people, hides in corners, and generally seems uncertain of life, new owners tend to think she's been beaten. Not always true. In our experience, raising a dog in isolation is a much more common cause of these particular problems.

Your first instinct may be to baby these mistreated mutts in an effort to compensate for all the wrong perpetrated against them. Don't. What they need most is calm, sane handling by a calm, sane leader. They do not need to be left to their own unstable devices by a cooing, confusing nonleader.

Curing Hand Shyness

Your new companion can be reconditioned not to fear your hands. To do this you must stop any and all hitting of the dog, then desensitize him to the hitting motion so he no longer cringes from it.

Desensitizing a dog is a relatively simple process, although it may take some time to accomplish. Start with a piece of cherished food in one hand. It has to be something your dog is wild for. Don't be shy here, a biscuit isn't adequate. It has to be special—only given in these sessions. It has to be spectacularly enticing. Your dog's eagerness for it will help him overcome his fear. Hold a small piece of the treat in one of your hands, in front of his nose. As he's sniffing and licking it, slowly raise your other hand over his head. If he accepts this movement without worry, give him the treat. Use lavish praise whenever your dog shows confidence.

If he is anxious anytime you stand near him with your arm up, try kneeling or sitting on the floor at first. Few dogs have been abused by a kneeling or sitting person, so they won't fear those positions. Make sure you keep talking to the dog in an enthusiastic voice throughout.

Repeat this procedure, slowly increasing the speed with which you raise your hand. Once he tolerates this without a flinch, move to the second level. Now, do not hold the treat to his nose. Instead, while a step or two away from the dog, raise your hand without the treat slowly over your head and *slowly* step toward him. As you near him, give him the treat with the other hand while you lower the raised arm down to stroke his head. Praise enthusiastically!

A little trick that helps this type of dog is to back up a step or two every time he takes the treat. Not only will your retreat give him confidence, but it releases any stress he may feel in being close to you and allows him to approach you again for the next round.

Over many sessions, increase the speed of the hand raising and the step toward the dog. Always follow this with a treat and much praise. Your dog will learn to have no fear of you or your hand motions. Stay relaxed. This type of training takes as long as it takes. Some dogs will relax completely in two weeks, others in two months. It's not a race.

Dogs who make no progress after several sessions need the help of a professional trainer or behavioral counselor. Dogs who are movement-sensitive in general need to be carefully socialized with children and always supervised. They have experienced the worst humans have to offer. Don't forget that: they won't. With these dogs it is always better to allow them to approach a person rather than the person approaching them. No approach, no interaction.

Never soothe or console a dog for showing fear. Phrases like "It's okay" only make his fear worse. Instead of making him feel better, you'll actually be rewarding fearful behavior. Anything you reward will happen more—not less. Instead, reward him anytime he shows confidence and you'll see more of it.

Your dog looks to you for guidance. A simple rule is: your dog reflects your emotions. If you are happy and confident, he is more likely to be. If you are worried and anxious, he is more likely to be that too!

Physical Abuse: Case Study

Meeting Ci was a damp experience. Every interaction was, to put it kindly, damp. A more truthful description would be wet. Ci had a massive submissive urination problem that the man in the family had given him. Ci—short for Homicide—was a Black Lab mix of some kind, a sweet and gentle soul adopted by a family in Brooklyn. The father of the family had hoped for some big, tough, guard breed mix. The best he could find was a floppy-eared, big-footed black pup. The terrible name was attached in the hopes he would grow into it. He didn't.

As Ci—as I much prefer to call him—grew, his sensitive nature became apparent. This sweetness disgusted the man, who backhanded the dog whenever he groveled. This aggression increased the pup's submission. He desperately tried to please his human by belly-crawling, rolling on his back, and, soon enough, urinating—a clear canine white flag. Submissive urination, a leftover from puppy behavior toward the mother, is a canine signal of surrender, a plea to stop all aggression.

This new turn of events enraged the man, who was quite sure the pup was doing this to spite him. The backhands turned into more—more force, more often, more pain. Ci fell completely apart. Soon he was urinating whenever any human walked into the room, looked his way, or spoke to him.

Dr. Mike McGuill shows proper body position while hand-feeding a timid dog.

RECLAMATION

To turn this around, if it can indeed be turned around, will probably take a long time with no mistakes on your part.

Hand Feeding

Feeding the dog completely from your hand is a nice way to reestablish the bond. It also gives you wonderful opportunities for play training, which helps build any dog's trust.

No *Verbal or Physical Corrections*

Problem behavior is to be either ignored or redirected. Soon, instead of fearing the consequences, the dog will relax. Once relaxed he can learn what you want him to do. As soon as that stage is reached, things will progress steadily.

Ignoring Behavior

Any correction of any kind will make this problem worse! Greet the dog outside, ignore him for the first ten minutes when you get home, have guests ignore him too. Ignoring him will take the pressure out of the situation, allowing the dog to relax.

Teach Him

Teaching him exactly what you want him to do is a wonderful way of reducing his stress. Commands like sit, stay, or place (meaning go to your bed and stay there for a while) are terrific tools. They increase his self-control, relax him, and further build the bond between you.

Develop Routines

Every day you come home. Every day you ignore him. Every day he gets a biscuit. Every day you go out for a walk. Routines mean predictability. Predictability means the dog can relax. He knows exactly what the day holds. A relaxed dog is a drier dog.

Develop routines he can hold to at certain stressful times, like when people enter your home. Have friends help you with this. Have them toss him a treat as they enter. Once he can handle this, allow him to approach them to receive his treat. Make sure your friend does not look at or speak to the dog during this phase. A few practice sessions like this and your dog will greet people in a relaxed, happy, and dry manner.

Solving the Top Mutt Behavior Problems

Some mutts are born problem-free. Most can be made problem-free, but it takes an investment on your part. Investment of your time—learning how to handle the problem; energy—handling the problem; faith—that the problem can be resolved; and dedication—to follow through. Owner commitment is an incredible thing; we've seen it turn around dogs for whom we had little hope.

This section gives you the fundamental information you need to handle common canine behavior problems. We are giving you the most effective tools for training or retraining a dog, but like all tools, none is right for every dog with every owner in every situation. If you try one method and it is not effective, give up on the method, not on the dog.

This section does not deal with aggression. Although aggression is an all-too-common dog problem it is not a fix-at-home, do-it-yourself type of problem. If your dog shows signs of aggression of any kind seek professional help immediately. Aggression does not "get better" on its own. Aggressive dogs can be managed through training and careful handling but they will rarely be 100 percent "cured." When you relax the rules, expect to see the old problem rear its ugly head. In light of this, we feel it is not appropriate for us to give you a short course on this problem. Please refer to the Training Resources section in the Bibliography for books offering more detailed instruction. Good luck.

INAPPROPRIATE CHEWING

Causes

- #### BOREDOM/LACK OF EXERCISE
The more intelligent your mutt is, the more likely she is to become bored. Dogs are social, active creatures. If yours spends most of her time alone while getting little exercise or training when you are home, expect her to amuse herself in ways you may not find amusing. Mutts, especially young animals of active breed mixes, need a great deal of exercise to be calm. If you don't have access to a fenced-in area, use a long line to give your mutt room to stretch her legs.

- #### LACK OF APPROPRIATE TOYS
Chewers will chew. All you can hope to accomplish is making sure they chew acceptable objects. Supplying plenty of good toys like hard nylon bones, sterilized real bones, rubber toys, and big rope toys offers excellent outlets for your dog's urges.

- #### PLEASURE
For dogs, chewing is fun. Chewing things that smell like you, are easily ripped into tiny bits, or can be unstuffed are incredible fun.

- #### ANXIETY
Just as smokers tend to smoke more when upset, chewing dogs tend to chew more when they're upset. If you've had a history of getting angry at your dog and the chewing is getting worse, anxiety is

TRAINING BASICS

Fun

Fun is absolutely mandatory! If training isn't fun for you, you won't do it. If training isn't fun for the dog, he won't do it. Training is a wonderful excuse for us adults to romp, laugh, play, and otherwise have a good time. All compliance on the dog's part should be met with heartfelt enthusiasm on your part. You will be amazed at how effective it is.

Fair

Part of being a leader worth following is being consistent with your expectations and clear in your desires. Do you repeat commands? Easy habit. Bad habit. Every time you repeat yourself, you are saying to the dog, I don't know what I want, you can ignore me. Is that fair? When you get angry at him for not listening, whose fault is it if you've been repeating yourself all the time? Are you guilty of changing the commands? Most people are. "Sit," "Sit Down," "Sit,sit,sit,sit!" all sound completely different. Before you blame the dog, ask yourself: "Have I been 100 percent consistent? Have I practiced? Have I been changing the words I use?" Until you are sure that you are doing your part well, don't blame the dog for not doing his.

Firm

Firm means calm enforcement, no confusion, no fear, no pain, and no options. Firm does not mean anger, screaming, hurting, or terrifying. Simply put, firm means that "Sit" means lower your rear to the ground, right now. "Good dog!" Firm means you expect action—either his or yours. If he obeys—wonderful! Praise and celebrate. If he looks at you blankly, you enforce your command— calmly, evenly, and consistently. When a dog can count on your consistency without being confused by fear, he learns amazingly quickly.

Giving the dog plenty of the right things to chew helps prevent problems from developing.

Hope Ryden

probably the cause. See the section on Separation Anxiety for more help.

• TEETHING

Puppies get their adult teeth between four and six months of age. During that time painful gums can drive even a mild-mannered pup to gnawing a table leg.

• BREED MIX TENDENCY

Certain breeds have a reputation for being destructive. If your chewer has this parentage, congratulations! Your dog is simply acting out a piece of his true nature. Next time you find a chewed shoe on the floor, pick it up and say, "Yup, now we know you really *are* a Labrador mix!" Breeds who have a reputation for epic chewing include any kind of retriever,

Siberian Husky, Basenji, Australian Cattle Dog, Weimaraner.

Cures

• PREVENTION

When you are home, keep your dog in your sight, on leash next to you, or in a crate. Keep the door of the room you are in closed. This prevents your canine demolition expert from leaving without you noticing.

When you can't pay attention, confine him in a crate. Breaking the chewing habit by prevention is critical; crating accomplishes that. Crating also teaches your dog to sleep when left alone. Sleeping dogs don't chew. Please see Crate Training on the next page for further instructions.

• REDIRECTION

Supply plenty of desirable toys to chew on. Rotate the toys every few days. Rub a bit of cheese or butter into toys to encourage chewing. If you catch your dog even considering chewing the wrong thing, tell him to "Leave it!" in a calm, firm, no-nonsense voice and then direct him to a toy. "Get your ball? Where's your ball?" Go with him and get it if he doesn't know what you mean. Praise him warmly. He'll soon catch on.

• STRUCTURE

Good training builds confidence and establishes respect between you and your dog. Train him every day using positive, fun methods. Not only does this give your dog something to think about but it

CRATE TRAINING

Crate training is truly one of the greatest training tools ever invented. Used correctly, as any tool should be, it is humane and effective for most dogs. Used incorrectly by leaving a dog in it too long, not exercising the dog properly, or not introducing the crate properly, it can be a cruel tool. But then, hammers have been misused for any number of heinous crimes and I hardly blame the hammer.

Here are some basic do's and don'ts of crating your dog.

- Do remove all collars before crating your dog.

- Do leave the crate door open at first. Hide treats inside. This allows the dog to explore it at her own pace.

- Do feed her in the crate. First with the door open, later with it closed.

- Do introduce her gradually. Being put in and left for several hours will not endear the crate to her. Sometimes that is unavoidable, but it is not ideal.

- Don't reward barking and whining with release. This only trains him to bark and whine more!

- Do practice confinement in the daytime first. This allows you to work out the details without you, and possibly your unamused neighbors, being kept up half the night.

- Don't put bedding in with your new puppy or adult. A stressed animal can make confetti out of bedding. A dirty dog may use the absorbent material to mask his mistakes. Best just to skip it for the first month or so. The exception to this is a sight hound mix or other boney, thin-coated dogs—they need the padding to be comfortable.

- Don't put newspaper in the crate. You're trying to teach her not to go in there!

- Do crate her in the bedroom at night. She will be more contented if she is near you.

- Do practice crating while you are home. Otherwise it will become a signal of your leaving and cause stress in some dogs.

establishes your leadership. If you work him calmly for a few minutes before you leave, it may have a positive effect on the problem.

Common Mistakes

• CORRECTION AFTER THE FACT

Very common, very human—and wrong. In fact, will make him chew more! If you come home to destruction, shame on you! Why wasn't your dog crated? If you want to correct someone, give yourself a sound scolding but leave your dog out of it. Prevention, not correction, is your key to success.

• OVERLY EMOTIONAL DEPARTURES AND RETURNS

If you treat your dog when you come and go as you do your parents or spouse, you won't be too far off. Do you run up to your mother or husband saying, "It's okay, I'll be right back. Really honey, I'll be back in just a little while, it's okay. You be good, okay?" all the while stroking them nervously? No. At least we hope not. Mostly we are casual, "I'll be back in ten minutes, bye," and off we go. No big deal.

BARKING

Causes

• BOREDOM

More often than not, bored dogs are bad dogs. If your dog is barking too much, maybe she has nothing better to do. This is particularly true of "beacon barking,"

Scotch clearly thinks working with his owner, Gigi, is the best.

that annoying once-a-minute bark whose sole purpose seems to be to remind you that your dog is still there, in case you had forgotten.

• ALARM

Most of us want our dogs to sound the alarm, we just don't want them to keep sounding it or to hang out the front window barking at every bicyclist, squirrel, or truck that happens by.

• FEAR

Fear barkers often bark while moving backward, tail down, hackles up. The most common causes of this type of barking are an unidentified object (like a paper bag left in the living room) or a person at the door.

• DEMAND

This is an annoying one. Your dog barks for attention. Prime times for this onslaught are while you are watching TV, talking on the phone, or attempting intimacy with your spouse. The bad news is this type of barking is 100 percent *your fault*. The good news is—it's fixable.

• BREED-SPECIFIC

If your mix contains breeds selected for generations for their barking—such as scent hounds and terriers—do not be surprised when your dog is vocal. The Finnish Spitz, Pomeranian, Shetland Sheepdog, Bearded Collie, and Norwegian Elkhound are also legendary for their barking ability.

Cures

• REDIRECTION

Give her something else to do. If she's barking out the window, first tell her she's a "Good dog" for sounding the alarm. After all, alerting you is not wrong. Alerting you for twenty minutes is. Then have her "Come" and "Down/Stay."

If she knows the commands but ignores them, calmly insist she comply. Do not repeat yourself. Do not become upset. Remember to praise her warmly once she obeys, even if you had to make her respond.

Mieshka

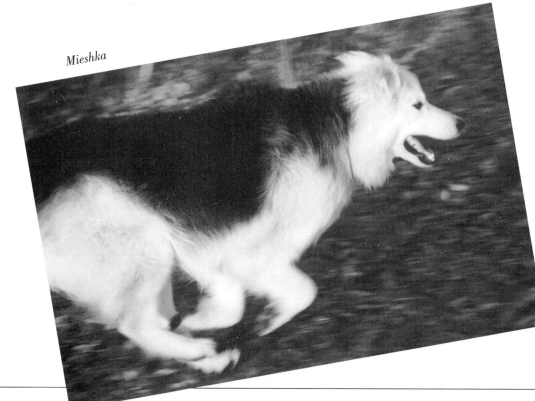

Don Kretzschmar

If the commands "Come" and "Down/Stay" are new to you both, work on them when all is quiet, or take her to a local training class and get some control. Then, leave a lead on her when you are home so you can enforce your commands if you need to. Be sure you praise her well for obeying. She deserves it.

A similar approach can be taken with demand barking. Give her all the attention she wants, in the form of commands—"Sit, Down, Sit, Down." This is one instance where you should withhold praise. We want to bore her. She'll soon connect barking at you with doing "command chores" and amuse herself in some other way.

• EXERCISE

This is the panacea for all canine behavioral ills. When in doubt, get her out! Being let out the back door is *not* exercise—if she isn't panting, she isn't working. (Note: Allow dogs under a year of age to set their own pace, as forced exercise at a young age can be harmful. Check with your vet for individual guidance.)

• PREVENTION

Interrupting the cycle of barking helps. Crate-training your dog calms many insecure barkers. Set up the crate in a bedroom. Leave a radio on to muffle any outside sounds that may set your dog off. Leaving an article of worn clothing in the crate is often comforting. Alternatively, if your dog will stay behind one, put a wire mesh gate across a doorway. This keeps your dog from running to the window to bellow at the neighbor's dog. Simply closing the door and preventing

your dog access to that area may work like a charm. Be creative—it can give you a quick solution.

• CORRECTION

If you are sure that you have addressed your dog's needs—physically and mentally—and she is still barking too much, then consider correction. But correction will only work if all other pieces are in place. Trying to stop a Beagle-Pomeranian mix from barking when she is left all day at home won't work if the only exercise she gets is three short bathroom walks along with no training or direction. Attend to her needs first; then, if the unwanted behavior still exists, correct it.

A series of enforced "Downs," the "Leave It" command and/or the judicious use of a shake can (see Booby Trap, page 193) may have good effect.

Common Mistakes

• BARKING BACK

As far as your dog is concerned, when you yell you are just joining in. Stay calm. Direct your dog's behavior, don't react to it.

• REWARDING THE BARKING

Who would be silly enough to do this? Most of us, though not on purpose. Here's an example: Your best friend comes to the door wearing an appalling new hat. Your dog, no longer recognizing this familiar face, explodes into spasms of barking. You get her by the collar and stroke her. "It's okay. It's only Mary-Anne," you coo soothingly.

Guess what? You just rewarded her. Be careful! Only reward behavior you want to see more of. Ignore, prevent, or correct behavior you want to go away.

Other examples of rewarding barking:

- Dog barks at the back door, you let her in.
- Dog barks at you while you're on the phone, you toss her a biscuit to quiet her.
- Puppy barks at a larger dog, you laugh at her boldness while you pet her.

Get the idea?

Rewarding sitting is a great way to help eliminate jumping.

JUMPING UP

Causes

- ### FRIENDLINESS

This is the most common cause of nuisance jumping. The scenario normally is: you come home, dog greets you as if you've been gone on a trip around the world.

- ### ANTICIPATION

If you are holding a tennis ball and your dog leaps on you for it, or tries to get to a dinner plate raised high above your head, then you are already familiar with anticipatory jumping.

Cures

- ### SETTING UP THE SITUATION

It's no real surprise, is it, that your dog jumps when you come in? He does it each and every time you open the door. Given this consistency on his part there is no reason for you not to be prepared.

- ### GIVING THE RIGHT ANSWER

What is it that you want from the dog? In this case it is to sit when greeting you. Do you tell him that? Do you reward him for sitting instead of jumping? Developing the desired behavior is much quicker and more fun than trying to eliminate the unwanted. If your dog sits when you come home, the jumping is solved. And your dog will get what he wants—your attention—while he hears "Good Dog!" instead of "No, stop it! Bad Dog!"

• GUIDE INTO CORRECT BEHAVIOR

If your mutt is a food hound or toy lover, use that to your advantage. Keep a favorite toy or treat outside the door. When you enter, command "Sit," then hold the toy or treat about a few inches above his head. When he sits, give him the treat or toss the toy a short distance. Do not reward him for jumping at it. Soon he'll be planting his bottom the minute you open the door. Practice this technique in a quiet area first. This way he'll do exactly what you want him to do when you hold a toy or treat this way.

• LEASH CORRECTION

Grasp the leash two feet away from your dog's collar and give a quick snap off to one side. You do not have to use a lot of force! Give yourself plenty of slack and be quick. Tugging hard or yanking at the collar won't work well.

A dog on two legs is poorly balanced; even a small sideways pressure will force him onto all fours. Be sure to praise your dog for getting off his hind legs.

• NOISE CORRECTION

For many dogs, the proper use of a startling sound can make an excellent training tool. Like all training tools it is not appropriate for all dogs nor is it effective if misused. Many gun dog crosses are not impressed by sound corrections, having been selected for generations to tolerate the noise of gunfire without a blink. Do not use these techniques on shy or sound-sensitive dogs (thunderstorm haters).

That said, noise corrections are easy to do. Leave a shake can (see p.193) outside your door or keep a throw chain in your pocket. When you enter, tell your dog "Off," then "Sit." If he complies, great! Praise him. If he does not, give the can a brisk shake behind your back or toss the throw chain down at the floor near his hind feet. The can may also be tossed to the floor if the behind-the-back shake is not effective. At no time should the can be shaken at the dog or should anything be thrown at the dog.

The moment he gets off his hind legs, praise him calmly while he is sitting. After a few days of this, he'll get the idea.

• IGNORE THE DOG

In some cases, simply crossing your arms and looking at the ceiling will cause the dog to stop. He is trying for your attention; if he isn't getting it, some dogs will sit down in puzzlement. The moment he does sit, praise him calmly. If he jumps, ignore him again. This may take a few minutes at first, but he may well get the idea quickly. Clearly this is not the technique to use with a large, powerful dog—after all, training is not supposed to be painful for either of you.

Common Mistakes

• INCONSISTENCY

Maybe the truth is that you actually like the jumping—some of the time. Maybe on the weekends, when you are wrestling or when you come home from a hard day, the jumping seems like love, play, and fun. Or perhaps you are the picture of consistency but the rest of your family reward his hind leg hopping. If you and your family can't be consistent, how can you expect your dog to be consistent?

• CREATING PAIN, NOT UNDERSTANDING

The age-old methods of solving jumping blame the dog. Instead of teaching him what he should be doing or controlling ourselves before we turn to the dog, these methods are based on hurting the animal. These unacceptable methods advocate kneeing him, stepping on his toes, or squeezing his paws. We call this "hurt him till he stops" dog training.

In some cases, those methods may work but the ends do not justify the means. There are better ways. Since it is you who created this problem, why hurt the dog?

HOUSEBREAKING MISTAKES

Causes

• YOUTH

Puppies are not born with control over their bodily functions any more than babies are. Luckily for dog owners, puppies quickly develop control, most having excellent abilities to hold their urine and bowels by four to five months.

Before that, however, expecting a pup to keep clean is futile. Some miraculous pups do seem to get control early, but don't count on it. A clean house before the age of self-control is your job. Supervision, routine, and prevention are the keys.

• OLD AGE

As your companion gets older, she may need to go out more frequently than before. If your older dog starts having accidents, take her to the vet for a checkup. If all is well, simply increase her daily walks. For heaven's sake, don't scold her. She probably is mortified enough already.

• CHEMICAL IMBALANCE

If your mix, usually a spayed female, urinates in her sleep, get her to the veterinarian. This is often a sign of a fairly common chemical imbalance that is usually easily controlled with medication.

• CONFUSION

Some mistakes are simply due to confusion. Classically this is the young or small dog who has been paper-trained in the past and now the owner is attempting to get her to go outside. Dutifully, the animal holds every drop in until you return home, at which point she runs to her old potty area and relieves herself. Don't blame her! She's just doing what she thinks you want.

• HABIT

Some dogs develop a favorite spot to relieve themselves. Normally this is a location they consider ideal: private, not frequently used. Formal dining rooms, under a piano, behind a potted plant, or in the basement all fit this description nicely. Alternative locations are the room of the lowest-ranking pack member, often the youngest child, or near the back door.

• MARKING TERRITORY

If your dog is lifting his leg in your house he does not have a housebreaking

Emma needs instructions, not punishment.

Shelley Singer

Most of the tiny mixes, through no fault of their own, take a bit longer to catch on. The house is just proportionally so much larger for them that it takes more consistent care to get them on track. Also, small dog stools are less offensive to most people, so they shrug it off longer. Most of our clients don't call us with tiny-dog housebreaking complaints till well over a year. By that time getting them back on track is no short-term task.

Any mix of the pack hounds—Beagles and Bassets being the most common— can be hard to get clean. Some of the Nordic breed mixes—like Husky crosses—can take a little longer, and we've seen a discouraging number of male Soft-Coated Wheatens who take months of careful management to catch on.

problem. He's a leg lifter and that's entirely different. As that leg goes up, respect for you goes down. A leg lifter can walk five miles, go to the bathroom fifteen times, yet still hike his leg against the couch. Why? Not because he has a full bladder, more because he is full of himself. Leg lifting is hard to stop, so you'll have to set your mind that you're going to succeed and keep at it until you do!

Leg lifters have to be neutered before you're going to make any headway at all. Read the section on the Demanding Dog (page 186) and follow every step. Then get both of you into a good local class or find a qualified local trainer or behaviorist for private work.

Cures

• ROUTINE

The more consistent you are about what and when your dog eats, drinks, and walks, the more consistent your dog will become about when and where she relieves herself.

• SUPERVISION

This means both inside and outside. It is all too easy to let your dog out into the fenced backyard when it's raining while you stay inside warm and dry. But if you do this you won't notice your dog sitting miserably on the back step, never doing what you thought she was doing. Then when she answers nature's call under your dining room table you blame her. Wrong! Supervision is supervision, convenient or not.

• GOING ON COMMAND

Dogs have no embarrassment about urinating or defecating. Because of that, it is pretty simple to teach them a command that means "Here, Now!" Every time they squat or hike their leg calmly tell them "Hurry Up." After they finish, praise them and give a treat. Over a period of time—days for some dogs, weeks for others—they will learn to relieve themselves on command.

• CONFINEMENT

Most dogs have an inborn desire to keep where they sleep and eat clean. It's amazing to watch tiny pups just a few weeks old toddle over to the far side of their living area to relieve themselves. All housebreaking is built on this instinct.

If your dog is dirty in the house, crate-train her, confine her in a small room with a gate, or keep her next to you on lead when you are home. Don't tether your dog when you are away. Tethering is dangerous. We've seen dogs who have almost lost their legs after they became tangled. A crate is much safer for your dog.

• PROPER CLEANING

Clean all mistake areas, even if you can't see any residue, with an odor neutralizer. These specially designed products can be purchased at your veterinarian or pet supply store. The canine nose is miraculous, capable of smelling one part salt in a million parts water. Vinegar and water won't do the trick. If she can smell where she went previously, she'll be attracted back there.

• DINING IN THE BATHROOM AGAIN?

After cleaning, feed your dog in the area she messed. No one, dogs included, likes to dine where they relieve themselves.

• STACKING THE DECK

If you have a dog who refuses to go outside, try this little trick. On a nice day, when you have several hours that you wouldn't mind spending outside, stack the deck in your favor. Mix up a few cups of warm water and wet food, or chicken broth or anything that your dog is likely to drink to excess. Allow her to drink her fill and more. Now go outside with her.

It will take a bit, maybe even an hour, for the bladder to become undeniably demanding, but it will. It's the canine equivalent of drinking four to five cans of soda. She will go to the bathroom.

When she finally does let go, praise her calmly as she is going, then party wildly when she is through. Praise her, pet her, give treats—don't leave any doubt in her head what you want.

Then stay out a bit longer, as she'll need to go a couple more times before all the liquid is out of her system. Normally, once a dog has gotten praised for relieving herself outside once or twice, she gets the idea.

Common Mistakes

• LOSING YOUR TEMPER

Losing your temper teaches your dog to fear you but doesn't do anything for her understanding of housebreaking.

• RUBBING YOUR DOG'S FACE IN HER MESS

Disgusting and useless. We love the argument that dogs got housebroken because of this barbaric habit. *No.* The dog got housebroken because most dogs want to be housebroken and eventually do become housebroken despite what we do to them, not because of this disgusting old training myth.

• LACK OF SUPERVISION

Treat any puppy under seven months of age and any adult dog with a history of making mistakes like a toddler without a diaper on. Keep them in sight! With a dog, you can close the door so she stays in the room with you, keep her on lead next to you, or confine her to a crate if you can't watch her.

SUBMISSIVE URINATION

These sweet dogs urinate when they get excited. Prime times for this are when you, or anyone else, enters your home or if you scold them. This has nothing to do with housebreaking. It is actually an extremely polite canine gesture of respect. Many pups will do this and, if you don't react to it, most will outgrow it.

Causes

• EXCITEMENT

When submissive wetters get excited, they piddle. Some urinate a little, some grace you and the surrounding areas with a pool.

• INTIMIDATION

If your dog has been intimidated in the past either by you or a previous owner, he is peeing in an effort to avoid punishment in the future. This type of submissive urination is usually person-linked, many times to men or to a particular male.

• BREED MIX

Some mixes, American Cocker Spaniel in particular, are prone to this problem.

Liz Sharpe

Leaky Peter, seen here conversing with a friend, recovered from an early submissive urination problem—but it's hard to shake those childhood nicknames. Read more about him on page 82.

Cures

• IGNORING

If you know your dog's trigger situations, then a straightforward solution is to just ignore your dog when you are in these situations. And we do mean ignore—no eye contact, no speaking to, no touching. Just go about your day as if nothing is happening, and hopefully it won't be.

If your dog is a doorway puddler, instruct guests to ignore your dog for the first ten minutes or so when they are at your house.

• FOOD DISTRACTION

It is hard to be fearful and anticipatory at the same moment. Distracting the dog with a biscuit when you enter the house can avoid mishaps. Keep a stash by the door and when you enter, toss one to your dog. Ignore the dog and continue. Over time, your dog will come to look forward to you coming home, instead of being anxious about it.

• COMMAND TRAINING

Training, which focuses on praise and enthusiasm, builds canine confidence. If your dog knows exactly what you want, exactly how to please you, and exactly what wonderful thing will happen when he does, he will have no doubts. A dog with no doubt about what a human will do is a dry dog.

Common Mistakes

• CORRECTING THE DOG

Correcting a dog for submissively urinating is like throwing gasoline on a fire to put it out. The only way to solve this problem is to ignore it, train your dog using positive methods, and wait. Over time, it will decrease. Slip once and yell at him, and it will take you twice as long next time to get him dry.

PULLING ON LEAD

Cause

• LACK OF EFFECTIVE TRAINING

Dogs learn to walk politely on lead because they are trained to do so. It is not a natural canine reaction, as demonstrated by the hundreds of thousands of dogs who take their owners out for a daily drag. No dog is exempt from this problem, although some scent hound, retriever, and Nordic mixes are Olympic-class yankers.

Cures

• EFFECTIVE TRAINING

Most dog owners give an earnest, if unproductive, attempt at stopping this behavior. As you probably have already discovered, walking down the street yanking on your dog while repeating "Heel, heel, heel" doesn't get you anywhere. The reason this doesn't work is that you are not making yourself clear to your dog.

For your dog to learn, he has to understand why it's worth doing. This education can be approached in a couple of different ways. These different methods can be used individually or combined, depending on your dog and your own preference.

• LEASH WORK

This is a complex subject. We refer you to a local training class or professional for hands-on instruction. If that is not available, the books and videos in the Training Resources section of the Bibliography contain detailed information.

Seconds ago this dog was out of control—not anymore. And he's happy about it, too.

Jim Kalett

Regardless of where you learn, no dog should be flipped over or airborne during any part of this teaching. Such things are the result of too much force, bad timing, poor technique, or all three. If this happens during your training sessions, find someone to help you. If you've hired someone who does this, find someone else.

• FOOD REWARD/PLAY TRAINING

This involves using a desired object—food or a toy—to get your dog's attention. This work is done incrementally, starting with just a step or two of "Heel" rewarded immediately with the toy or treat. Over time the behavior is built up until the dog can work with good control over long distances. This is a good concept, but not so easy in real life. We tend to use these techniques in combination with good leash work to motivate the dog and the handler with some fun!

• HEAD HALTERS

Head halters for dogs are excellent management tools. While they do not train your dog not to pull, they do effectively prevent him from doing so. It takes a few days to a week for most dogs to accept a halter, but once they learn to accept it, it's smooth sailing.

Common Mistakes

• NOT PRACTICING ENOUGH

Think of this work as an investment in the comfort of both you and your dog. It can't be pleasurable or good for him to be choking himself on every outing. It isn't good for you to be yanked about either.

Here's what a head halter looks like on.

is behaving well in a calm environment, slowly begin exposing him to more distractions. Start with the distraction far enough away so that your dog doesn't get overly excited. Work there until he can calmly accept the temptation, then move a bit closer and work some more. Over a period of weeks, he'll soon be able to control himself in the face of five squirrels doing the rumba down your sidewalk.

• Not Believing It Can Work

You must believe. If you don't, your dog won't either. Be decisive. The clearer you are about what you want, the easier it is for your dog to give it to you.

The Demanding Dog

Causes

• You

You love your dog. You feel sorry for her that her life had a hard start. Every time your dog comes to you, putting a paw on your knee while nudging your hand for a pat, you feel flattered. After all, she just wants some loving reassurance, right?

Wrong! When you pet a dog who has nudged you, you are not saying "I love you" to the dog, you are actually saying "I obey you." The dog gave you a clear command—"Owner, pet me *now*!" and you complied. Ten points for the dog, zero for you.

Complying with such demanding behavior is a first step toward your dog ignoring you, or worse. Ah, I can hear it from here: "But she's just being sweet." "What harm could it do?" Let's translate

If you do this work for a few minutes every walk, or even once a day, you will be surprised just how quickly he catches on. One of the mightiest forces in the universe is a devoted owner with her mind made up. Decide right now that this is not going to continue and I promise you, it won't!

• Not Working Around Distractions

You already know what sets your dog off—maybe it's squirrels or bicycles or the neighbor's dog barking at him, but whatever it is, it's human nature to try to avoid it. Wrong approach. Once your dog

Simply having your dog sit when she asks for attention goes a long way to controlling her behavior.

this into human terms for the moment, to clarify. What if a child came up to you and demanded "Hug me now!" and you did. If you refused, the child whined louder, tugging on your sleeve, "Mommy, hug me— now!" Is this cute behavior? Is the child being loving to you?

Now, imagine further that you do hug the child, on command, ten, twenty, even thirty times a day. (How many times do you pet your dog, on her command?) How might this affect your child's view of you?

Of course, if your dog is listening to you perfectly and has no behavior problems, by all means, relax and comply to the occasional canine command. But chances are, if you are even reading this section, that is not the case. Fortunately,

it is not hard to turn such behavior around.

• INSECURITY

Insecure dogs can really pull on your heartstrings. The temptation is to try to make their world better by giving them lots of attention. Nice idea but wrong. It actually makes them more insecure. Dogs need, crave, and must have clear direction to be relaxed. Instead of obeying your insecure dog's commands, have her obey yours. That will really make her feel better.

• DOMINANCE

Many dogs rise through the ranks in their homes with a nose nudge. Try this: ignore the nudge. If she becomes increasingly insistent, pawing you or even barking, she probably has some kind of dominance problem.

• BEEN TRAINED TO DO THIS

By petting her every time she nudges you, you have actually trained her to do this.

Cures

• GIVE HER ATTENTION, JUST NOT THE KIND SHE WANTS

The next time your friend commands you to pet her, "Down" her. Insist that she comply. Release her with an okay and "Down" her again. Release her and "Down" her again. Then go back to what you were doing.

• LIMIT YOUR ATTENTION

No more than ten minutes of attention per hour. When you interact with her, make it count! If the dog has you this well trained, she's plenty bright. Teach her tricks, make her think. Establish your leadership in positive ways.

• INCREASE HER EXERCISE

All this change is stressful for her. Giving her a positive outlet will relax her, making the transition from queen back to dog easier for all concerned.

Common Mistakes

• GIVING IN

You try to be strong but by the tenth nose nudge, you weaken. This is the worst thing you can do. By giving in after ten, you have now trained her to nudge you at least ten times.

• IGNORING THE GOOD/REWARDING THE BAD

Every one of us has done this at some point. Here's the classic scenario: Dog enters room and sits in front of you as you read the newspaper. You ignore her. She whines a bit and she nudges you. "What do you want, sweetie?" you say warmly as you stroke the soft hair behind her ears. She looks at you adoringly. Lies at your feet quietly. You go back to reading the paper.

What did the dog just get attention for? If you said whining and nudging you are right. Quiet sitting and lying at your feet got her nothing. Just reverse this

scene. She comes and sits in front of you. You stroke her and tell her how good she is. She whines and nudges you, you ignore her. She tries again, you "Down" her, then praise her briefly for complying. Now you're on the road to a less obnoxious pet.

NOT COMING WHEN CALLED

If your dog does not come to you when you call, you are not alone. Most dogs don't, but it doesn't have to be that way.

Causes

• LACK OF TRAINING

Of all the commands, this is the most important and the one the least carefully taught. Most dogs get little to no formal training on coming when called. They are just called when they are off lead, having fun running around. And we wonder why this doesn't work well.

• PUNISHING THE DOG FOR COMING

Punishment is anything your dog doesn't enjoy. If you call him from a romp in the backyard and bring him inside, in his eyes he's just been punished. He's playing with a favorite dog buddy and you call him. He comes, you clip on the lead—guess what he thinks? You discover a chewed shoe in your dining room, you call him. He comes to you and you scold him—what do you think he learns?

If something less than pleasant has to happen, go get your dog. At the very least,

call him to you, praise him for at least ten seconds for coming, and then take him inside, clip on the lead, or drag him to the tub for a bath.

Cures

• STEP-BY-STEP TRAINING

Put your dog on lead. Practice having him come and sit on a short lead first. If he won't do that, what makes you think he'll listen from across the yard? When you are home, leave the lead on him. When he is napping, chewing a toy, or barking out the window pick up the lead and have him come. Reward him for complying, even if you have to make him. Play with him, give him a treat, rub his belly—a reward is anything he really enjoys. Be creative, he'll love it!

Once he gets good at working on a short lead, graduate to a longer one. If you reward him well for coming, "Come" will soon be one of his favorite commands.

• PRACTICE

If you can find ways to make this fun for both of you, you will practice more. If you practice more, you will both get better at it. There is no shortcut, no substitute for good time well spent.

Common Mistakes

• FAILURE TO TRAIN

With all the other demands on our time, it can be hard to find a moment to train your dog. Fortunately, it doesn't take long.

The Do's and Don'ts of Adding a Second Dog

Do get a dog of the opposite sex. Opposite sex pairings are less likely to develop aggression problems.

Do get a much younger dog. The more difference in age there is between the dogs the less likely there is to be competition.

Do select a complementary temperament. If your first dog is a bit bossy, choose a more submissive companion.

Don't mix dogs wildly different in size. Mixing a tiny Chihuahua mutt with a hulking Lab-Dane cross is asking for accidental injury.

Slip in a minute or two as you wait for the water to boil for tea, or during the commercials of your favorite TV shows. A few minutes daily make a huge difference.

• SETTING YOURSELF UP FOR FAILURE

If you know darn well your dog doesn't come reliably when called, then don't set yourself up for a problem by letting him off the leash.

SEPARATION ANXIETY

Separation anxiety is a common problem with abused, abandoned, and adopted animals. This problem is described as a dog who is stressed when you leave. They can show this stress by chewing, barking, digging at the door, making housebreaking mistakes, or simply panting so heavily that they soak their front legs with saliva. The good news is that most separation anxiety can be dealt with through structure, exercise, emotional control on your part, and confinement on his.

Causes

• INAPPROPRIATE OWNER RESPONSE

The two most common owner responses to this type of behavior are coddling or getting angry. Both are equally nonproductive. Coddling rewards the dog for neurosis, making more neurosis likely in the future; anger only makes the anxiety worse, making anxiety more likely in the future.

• BOREDOM

Dumb dogs, bless their limited souls, cruise through life—questioning nothing,

For this dog, a feline friend was just what he needed.

Ninon Hutchinson

worrying about nothing. They may not win the Nobel Peace Prize, but they rarely cause any trouble either. Then there is the canine Einstein, the mix you thought you wanted and, fortunately or unfortunately, actually got. This dog doesn't cope well when left alone eight hours a day, five days a week. He solves great canine mysteries like "How does the refrigerator door open?" and "What's actually inside those couch cushions?" This dog needs things to do! Train him! Teach him Frisbee, agility, obedience, tricks. Exercise him, and when you're done, hire someone else to exercise him some more. Consider getting him a companion, perhaps a calm dog or laid-back cat.

• STRESS

Second-home dogs frequently have a history of being misunderstood and mishandled. They have been punished after the fact for barking, housebreaking mistakes, or chewing, which taught them to dread both the owner leaving and the owner returning home. This fear causes stress, which causes them to act out more.

• DISTURBANCE

Even a usually calm dog can fall to pieces if there is an unusual event in the middle of his day. Don't be surprised if the day the UPS man came, or the rugs in the corridor of your building were cleaned, or the maintenance crew cut tree limbs on your block, you come home to a small disaster. If your dog has a lapse like this after months of no problems don't despair. Just put her back on a strict routine with confinement for a few days: she'll get right back into the swing of things.

• MONDAY-TUESDAY SYNDROME AND NIGHT-OUT SYNDROME

Many dogs, especially dogs with separation anxiety, can't handle being alone all day and then having you go out at night. Even if your dog has been crated all day, crate him again when you go out. Be sure to exercise him well in between but don't leave him loose. Some of my clients even hire baby-sitters for their dogs if they are completely guilt-ridden about re-crating.

If your dog has problems on Mondays and Tuesdays, chances are the weekend's change in schedule is throwing him off. To help your dog over this, crate-train him and then keep a weekend routine similar to your weekday one. Give your dog most of his attention at the time you would on a workday. Confine him and ignore him during the time you would normally be at work. That way, when you leave for work on Monday, it won't be as stressful for him.

This same attitude applies to vacation time. A dog with separation anxiety can backslide badly after a holiday of constant companionship. Try to keep at least a semblance of his regular workday schedule. This is particularly important as the end of vacation draws near. Help him transition back into more time alone before you have to head back to work.

If your dog has fewer problems on Mondays and Tuesdays, but has a hard time later in the week, chances are the problems are exercise-related. Having gotten more exercise on the weekend, he is relaxed early in the week. Really good runs on Tuesday and Thursday may well help resolve this problem.

Cures

• CALM COMINGS AND GOINGS

Stay calm when you come and go. Emotional scenes will make matters worse for your dog. Treat your travels as the normal, everyday events they are. That will help your dog relax.

• CONFINEMENT

Many dogs who are anxious when alone benefit from confinement. This can be a crate or a gate keeping her in a small area. Notice that when she is frightened, she seeks out a small, enclosed space to curl up in. That's her way of comforting herself. Properly set up and introduced, confinement works. Please see the box on Crate Training on page 174.

There are also dogs who panic at any type of confinement, never settling down in the least. If this is your dog, discuss the matter with your veterinarian. There are drug therapies available that can help your dog learn to adjust. Many people don't like the idea of giving their dog drugs, but when it is necessary, the proper medication is a godsend. Please consider how uncomfortable your dog is being frightened so much of the time. If drugs can help her over that, great!

• PRE-LEAVING OBEDIENCE SESSIONS

About half an hour before you leave, take five minutes to do a calm obedience session with your dog. This sets her up to be relaxed when you leave.

• PRECAUTIONS

If your dog chews shoes, put your shoes away. This is no magic ultrasecret of the dog training world but . . . it does work. Buy trash cans with lids or store trash cans in a closet or under the sink. If little Fluffy leaves you presents in the guest room, put a spring on the door so it automatically shuts when you leave it. There is no shame in winning through prevention.

• STRUCTURE

Stay calm. First, structure the dog mentally by teaching him commands. Make him sit or down or stay or come anytime you deal with him. This type of strong, constantly reinforced leadership is calming to insecure dogs. Giving them constant attention and extra love only causes them to doubt your leadership, making them more anxious and more susceptible to stress when you leave.

With anxious dogs all teaching must be based on calm, positive methods. Yelling, hitting, or becoming impatient will only make things worse. Emphasize the positive, praise the good behavior, and take the time to teach the commands you want. You won't be disappointed.

Calm, enforced downs have a settling effect on many dogs.

Sarah Wilson

Common Mistakes

• OVEREMOTING

This covers many of the deadly sins of dog ownership—overcoddling, overcorrecting, and overexciting. Calm down!

• DENIAL

It constantly astounds us how many people call us with dogs who have been chewing for years, yet the owner still sounds surprised when they come home and find a mess. Your dog will change his behavior, but only after you change yours!

STEALING OBJECTS

Causes

• PLEASURE

One of the main reasons a dog steals things is that it gives her pleasure. She steals meat off the counter because it tastes good. She steals your socks out of the laundry because she thinks they smell great and because you chase her around the house in a most entertaining way.

• HUNGER

In rare cases, dogs are simply hungry and that is why they steal. Dogs who have previously been well mannered but start stealing after a food change are suspect. If your dog is thin, she may need more meals a day, bigger meals, or a worming. A trip to the vet is a good idea to make sure there is no underlying health problem.

Cures

• BOOBY TRAP

Since dogs mostly steal stuff because in one way or another it is fun, if you make it un-fun, she will stop. Shake cans work well for this. A shake can is an empty soda or beer can, rinsed out, with twelve pennies inside. (The pennies fit through the opening.) Make a few of these and set them on the counter. Tape thread to them and attach the thread to the object she still steal. Now wait. When she takes it the cans will fall from the counter, startling her. Once things start exploding when she takes them, she'll stop.

Environmental Corrections

An environmental correction happens to the dog when he attempts an unwanted behavior. You are not involved.
Examples: A shake-can booby trap. When your dog steals the dish towel, the cans "chase" him. Mousetraps under a piece of newspaper in the trash. Your dog sticks his nose in the can, the traps snap surprisingly, but harmlessly, under the paper (not recommended for homes with small children). Your dog puts his feet up on the counter, you silently lean around the corner and spray him with a water gun. You hide, he doesn't know who did it.
Different things work with different dogs, but something works with almost all of them.

Shelly Kintish

Honey is only trying to reach her own toys, but the next countertop involved a whole leg of lamb.

- **SETUP**

If you know your dog likes to steal dish towels, set her up. When you are home, leave a ten-foot piece of rope on her, then leave a dish towel hanging temptingly over the edge of the counter. When she takes it, casually step on the rope, then tell her "Out." Being in complete control eliminates her running off and allows you to reward her the instant she drops it.

- **PRAISE FOR DROPPING IT**

No matter how angry, frustrated, or disgusted you are you *must* praise your dog when she drops the item. Once she has the thing in her mouth it is too late to teach her not to steal it; the only thing you can effectively do now is teach her to drop it immediately. Once you are clear about that, then praising her for obeying is easy. Think of all the time it will save you running around the house after her.

Common Mistakes

- **PUNISHING AFTER THE FACT**

Doesn't work, give it up. If it was effective your dog would have stopped making the mistake, right? And you wouldn't be reading this section, right?

- **PUNISHING COMPLIANCE**

One more time: if your dog drops what's in her mouth, you must praise. If you do not praise, she will take just as long to drop it next time. If you get angry, your dog will take longer to drop it next time or she may elect to become aggressive, since she has no way of stopping your rage. Praise her wildly for dropping it and she will drop it faster next time. That is what you want, isn't it?

HYPERACTIVITY

The good news is very few dogs are actually hyperactive. Most simply display this behavior due to confusion and excess energy. Putting them on the right road is not hard and certainly much easier than living with an overly active dog.

Causes

- **REACTIVE**

Many, even most, hyperactive dogs are reactive dogs. If your dog gets more frantic when you correct him, if he runs around the house like a mad dog when you try to calm him down, if he jumps desperately at your face when you attempt to stop him—he's reactive. Simply put,

reactive dogs react to you. You get upset, they get upset. You get frantic, they get more frantic. Until you learn how to handle these dogs, they can drive you to drink.

Handling them effectively is a matter of staying calm (easier said than done at times) and directing them to the desired behavior instead of locking horns over the "bad" behavior. Praise should be abundant but calm. Do this and your dog will settle down amazingly quickly.

• LACK OF ADEQUATE EXERCISE

Already discussed many times in this section, so I won't spend more time on it here.

• INAPPROPRIATE FOOD

We have had experience with some dogs having a poor reaction to certain foods. While we are not qualified to venture a guess as to why, it does happen. If your dog gets more out of control after a food change, go back to what he was on before. If your dog has always been high-energy, try putting him on one of the many "natural" foods available. Occasionally, a simple food change can make an amazing difference.

• CONSTANT STIMULATION

Here's a problem unique to a big household. Everyone wants the dog's attention. Anytime he lies down for a nap, a kid runs over to play with him. Over time, he learns that humans want him to be active all the time. He actually becomes trained to be obnoxious. A good household rule is if the dog is being quiet and good—leave him alone. Whether he is napping, chewing a toy, or watching the kids play, leave him be. Interact with him only when he gets up and comes to you. This simple change in management can reap you huge rewards within a week.

Cures

• EXERCISE

Few problems respond to exercise as well as this one. There is no getting around it—get him out! Teach him to catch a Frisbee, pull a cart, carry three tennis balls in his mouth at once— whatever! But save yourself and him heartache and teach him something!

• DIRECTION

On his own, a hypractive dog will always make the wrong choices. Given five minutes to himself, he may empty the trash can, pull all the pillows off the

couch, or unravel the toilet paper. It's not his fault. Use your commands and use your head. Your job is to make sure you don't leave him in such a situation. Take him with you. Confine him safely. Give him a command. You have lots of options. Just don't blame the dog.

• RELAX!

Just because your dog is frantic doesn't mean you have to become frantic. Keep your voice calm and your mind focused. Don't waver in your goal of a calm, well-behaved dog. One of the quickest ways to get there is to stay calm and well-behaved yourself.

Common Mistakes

• PUNISHING HYPERACTIVITY

Hyperactive dogs can't control their behavior by themselves, they need your help. Yelling, threatening, or hitting causes more confusion, leading to increased unwanted activity. Next time you've reached the end of your rope, crate your dog, give him a new chew toy to work on, play ball with him for a few minutes, or tell him to "Down/Stay" for half an hour or so. These things will help him to control himself, not make him worse.

• REVVING THE DOG UP

If you are encouraging this behavior a few times a week by playing rough with him, getting him all excited, and wrestling with or teasing him, you are getting what you deserve—a dog who thinks hysteria is what you want. Remember: behave as you want your dog to behave. If your dog is overly active, you must behave calmly with much control. Chances are, he'll follow your lead.

BIBLIOGRAPHY

GENERAL DOG BOOKS

Benjamin, Carol Lea. *Second-Hand Dog*. New York: Howell Book House, Inc., 1988.

The original book on living with and loving an adopted dog, regardless of its heritage. This is a short, easy-to-read book with plenty of sensible advice.

Capuzzo, Michael. *Wild Things: The Wacky and Wonderful Truth About the Animal Kingdom*. New York: Ballantine Books, 1995.

Despite the title, this humorous and helpful book is mostly about cats and dogs and "is one of the most entertaining and useful pet books we've come across," said the American Humane Association.

Caras, Roger. *Roger Caras' Treasury of Great Dog Stories*. New York: E.P. Dutton, 1988.

A stirring collection from the dean of animal writers.

Caras, Roger. *The Roger Caras Dog Book*. New York: M. Evans & Co., 1992.

Caras, who loves dogs as much as any human ever has, evaluates the breeds with his classic, fireside-chat style, intelligence, and huge heart.

Comfort, David. *The First Pet History of the World*. New York: Fireside/Simon & Schuster, 1994.

Why didn't anyone think of this sooner? Comfort fills the niche with humor, insight, and zest.

Coren, Stanley. *The Intelligence of Dogs*. New York: The Free Press, 1994.

A useful, if controversial, look at canine gray matter, with bias favoring the breeds who do as told by humans.

Denenberg, R.V., and Eric Seidman. *The Dog Catalog*. New York: Grosset & Dunlap, 1977.

Dog history, literature, lore, and everything else you can think of.

Hamer, Lynne M. *Name That Dog: Dogs of Presidents, Kings, Queens, Governors, and Celebrities*. West Chester, Pa.: Animal Press, 1990.

A fun compendium of canine trivia.

Kelly, Niall. *Presidential Pets*. New York: Abbeville Press, 1992.

The authoritative, if brief, book on best friends and trusted canine advisers during two centuries at 1600 Pennsylvania Avenue.

Official Publication of the American Kennel Club. *The Complete Dog Book*. New York: Howell Book House, 1992.

Detailed, authoritative standards and excellent histories of every AKC-recognized breed of dog, leaving out only most dogs. Alas, no mutts allowed.

Winckur, Jon, comp. *Mondo Canine: A Treasury of Quotations, Anecdotes, Essays and Lore in Celebration of Doggie Joie-de-Vivre*. New York: E.P. Dutton, 1991.

A romp through canine lore.

Yamazaki, Tetsu. *Legacy of the Dog: The Ultimate Illustrated Guide to Over 200 Breeds*. New York: Chronicle Books, 1995.

Beautiful photographs and succinct breed profiles might help you to demystify your mutt's genealogy.

TRAINING RESOURCES

Kilcommons, Brian, and Sarah Wilson. *Good Owners, Great Dogs*. New York: Warner Books, 1992.

Comprehensive training and behavior book. Written for all ages and stages of dogs. Covers commands and has an extensive problem-solving section. Fun, easy to read and use, the methods work!

Kilcommons, Brian, and Sarah Wilson. *Good Owners, Great Dogs* (video)

A fine complement to the book, the dogs in this tape are straight out of the shelter. For both puppies and adult dogs, this fifty-seven-minute tape covers commands, problem prevention, and solutions to the most common behavior problems. The first tape to be recommended by the ASPCA.

Kilcommons, Brian, and Sarah Wilson. *Childproofing Your Dog*. New York: Warner Books, 1994.

Written for busy parents. Common sense, to the point and humane—a must read for anyone with both dogs and children in their life.

All Brian and Sarah's products, and more, are available through 800-457-PETS (7387).

Pryor, Karen. *Don't Shoot the Dog*. New York: Bantam Books, 1985.

This short, engaging book is a wonderful addition to any animal lover's library. Clearly shows the effectiveness of behavioral principles applied to real-life situations, be it with your dog or your spouse. Available through the Dog & Cat Catalog listed below.

Dog & Cat Catalog, Direct Book Service
Phone: 800-776-2665

They have EVERY book and video about dog behavior, selection, training, and care (over 2,000 titles). A must for any dog (and cat) lover!

Mixed Breed Organization
AMBOR (The American Mixed Breed Obedience Registration)
205 1st Street SW
New Prague, MN 56071
Phone: 612-758-4598

If you would like to earn obedience degrees with your mixed breed, or are interested in other forms of competition like agility or flyball, these are the people to contact.

MAGAZINES

Dog Fancy
PO Box 53264
Boulder, CO 80322-3264
Phone: 303-786-7306

Dog World
PO Box 5834
Harlan, Iowa 51593-0884
Phone: 800-361-8056

Good Dog!
PO Box 10069
Austin, TX 78766
Phone: 800-968-1738

Natural Pet Magazine
PO Box 351
Tribly, FL 33593-0351
Phone: 904-583-2770

PetLife: Your Companion Animal Magazine
1227 West Magnolia Avenue
Fort Worth, Texas 76104
Phone: 800-856-8060

NEWSLETTERS

Animal Health
Cornell University College of Veterinary Medicine
P.O. Box 52816
Boulder, CO 80322-2816
Phone: 800-873-2808

Your Dog
Tufts University School of Veterinary Medicine
PO Box 420272
Palm Coast, Florida 32142-0272
Phone: 800-829-5116

ACTIVITIES

Agility
USDAA (United States Dog Agility Association)
PO Box 850955
Richardson, TX 75085-0955

Frisbee
Flying Dogs
PRB & Associates
Suite 326F
4060-D Peachtree Road
Atlanta, GA 30319
Phone: 800-786-9240

THE source of soft, inexpensive flying discs as well as training information, regional competitions, and much more. The sport not only allows mixed breeds but is dominated by them.

Carting
Dog Works!
317 Curvin Drive
Stewartstown, PA 17363
Phone: 800-787-2788

Also good resource for Sledding, Hiking, and Water Work Equipment.

Sledding
Konari Outfitters, Ltd.
PO Box 752
52 Seymour Street
Middlebury, VT 05753
802-388-7447

Therapy Dogs
Alpha Affiliates, Inc.
Suite 362
103 Washington Street
Morristown, NJ 07960
Phone: 201-539-2770
Fax: 201-644-0610

Not a national registry, but they have excellent resources for those interested in pet-assisted therapy.

Delta Society
289 Perimeter Road East

Renton, WA 98055-1329
Phone: 800-869-6898 or 206-226-7357

Large, active organization. Offers a home study course and regional workshops. Well-respected national organization.

Therapy Dogs, Inc.
PO Box 2786
Cheyenne, WY 82003-2786
Phone: 307-638-3223

Excellent organization. Once you qualify, the only program that offers primary insurance coverage of their dogs and handlers.

Pet Sitters
National Association of Professional Pet Sitters (NAPPS)
Phone: 800-296-PETS

Here's an excellent resource for bonded professionals who can come to your home to care for your pet(s) when you are away.

Dog Identification

National Dog Registry
P.O. Box 116
Woodstock, NY 12498
Phone: 800-NDR-DOGS

This registry is tattoo based. Your dog is tattooed on his belly. This process is quick, with little—if any—discomfort. We've had many of our dogs tattooed. We highly recommend it as a positive and indisputable ID system. If your dog is ever stolen, he will not be used for laboratory research if tattooed.

Microchipping

Perhaps the wave of the future, perhaps not. At the time of this writing the technology has not sorted itself out, so different chipping systems do not work with other scanners, making the whole thing a mess. Personally, we like a visible, impossible-to-miss or -remove, user-friendly system like tattooing.

ID Tags

Fundamental ID that every dog should have. But because it is easily removed, not the only type of ID you should use.

ADOPTION

The American Humane Association, Englewood, CO 80112
Phone: 800-227-4645

To adopt a dog, find your local animal shelter in the phone book. The AHA receives complaints about local shelters and offers general information on dog care and other canine issues as well as disaster relief.

NATIONAL HUMANE ORGANIZATIONS

The American Humane Association, Englewood, CO 80112
Phone: 800-227-4645

American Society for the Prevention of Cruelty to Animals
424 East 92nd Street
New York, NY 10028
Phone: 212-876-7740

Humane Society of the United States
2100 L Street NW
Washington, DC 20037
Phone: 202-452-1100

To adopt a dog, go to your local shelter. For information on dog care and behavior, laws relating to dog and other domestic animals, and more—contact any or all of the above.

INDEX

ABOUT THE AUTHORS

BRIAN KILCOMMONS is a world-famous dog trainer and best-selling author, with Sarah Wilson, of *Good Owners, Great Dogs: A Training Manual for Humans and Their Canine Companions, Childproofing Your Dog,* and *Good Owners, Great Cats: A Guidebook for Humans and Their Feline Companions.* He has appeared on *Oprah, 20/20,* and PBS's *The Gentle Doctor: Veterinary Medicine.* Kilcommons is also a faculty member at the Tufts University School of Veterinary Medicine, and his clients include Diana Ross, Morley Safer, ASPCA President Roger Caras, Diane Sawyer, Marvin Hamlisch, among others.

MICHAEL CAPUZZO writes a syndicated column for *Newsday* and *The Philadelphia Inquirer* that was given the ASPCA President's Award for its "respectful and humorous stance toward animals." He is also the author of *Wild Things: The Wacky and Wonderful Truth About the Animal Kingdom.* A former feature writer for *The Philadelphia Inquirer,* Capuzzo has won the National Headliners Award and written for *Esquire, Sports Illustrated,* and *Life* magazine. As far as he knows, he is the only journalist nominated for the Pulitzer Prize who has won the Pawlitzer Prize, awarded by Alpo, for writing about Frisbee dogs.